body beauty & FOODS

body & beauty FOODS

MORE THAN 100 DELICIOUS RECIPES TO IMPROVE YOUR HEALTH,
BOOST YOUR IMMUNE SYSTEM, AND ENHANCE YOUR LOOKS

HAZEL COURTENEY & KATHRYN MARSDEN

RECIPES CREATED BY ANNE SHEASBY

Reader's Digest

THE READER'S DIGEST ASSOCIATION INC.
PLEASANTVILLE, NEW YORK • MONTREAL

The Library of Congress Cataloguing-In-Publication
data has been applied for.

ISBN 0-7621-0103-2

This book was conceived, designed and produced by
THE IVY PRESS LIMITED

Art Director: *Peter Bridgewater*

Editorial Director: *Sophie Collins*

Managing Editor: *Anne Townley*

Commissioning Editor: *Viv Croot*

Designer: *Clare Barber*

Project Editor: *Caroline Earle*

Editor: *Molly Perham*

Photography: *Marie-Louise Avery*

Printed in China

"*Let food be your medicine and medicine be your food.*"

HIPPOCRATES 469–399 B.C.E.

foreword

Most people recognize that we are made of what we eat. But many do not realize that by choosing the right foods, we can change the way we look and feel—both inside and out. This book clearly explains which foods are most beneficial, for what purpose and why. It identifies foods to encourage beautiful skin, hair, nails, and eyes, and foods that help boost immune function, maintain strong teeth and bones, and lead to more flexible joints and a healthier heart.

During the past five decades our diets and lifestyles have changed more radically than in the previous 2,000 years. Stress, pollution, pesticides, overuse of antibiotics and prescription drugs, plus a huge increase in the amount of fast foods we eat undoubtedly contribute to many health problems. But nutritional scientists and physicians now know that diet plays a role in many chronic conditions such as arthritis, eczema, gallstones, high blood pressure, cancer, and heart disease.

Many of the foods we eat consist of highly refined, mass-produced, prepackaged foods that often contain excessive amounts of salt, sugar, and chemical additives, such as preservatives and flavorings.

Unfortunately, many people talk about healthy eating, but in reality continue to eat poorly. Eventually this causes a deficiency in vital nutrients, overloads the system with toxins, and we become sick. Body & Beauty Foods helps to redress the balance toward better health. The body can often heal itself if given the right tools for the job. Food used properly and in the correct balance makes potent medicine.

We all have the freedom to choose what we put in our mouths, and if you want to become and stay healthier you need to make the right choices. If you are reading these words, you have already made a positive choice.

HAZEL COURTENEY

contents

beauty foods
104

introduction

Aim to eat at least five portions of fruit and vegetables a day for optimum nutrition.

The secret of a healthy diet is to forget the word "dieting." In fact, variety and balance are the keys to a lifetime of healthier eating. In this book Kathryn and I have selected many nutritious foods to help redress the imbalance of your diet with foods that heal rather than foods that harm. But don't panic—you can still enjoy your favorite treats. I'm sure you have heard the phrase "a little of what you fancy does you good"—but note the word little! When you eat something "bad," really enjoy it and don't feel guilty, but remember to keep a balance in all things and keep refined, sugary, fatty meals and treats to a minimum. It's hard, I know, because we are regularly bombarded with advertising that encourages us to eat more of the latest snack bar, prepackaged meal, or drink the latest drink—but these mass-produced foods and drinks may not have adequate nutritional value, and when eaten in excess, replace other wholesome foods in the diet and thus can deplete the body of vital nutrients.

Many people don't fully appreciate how diet can contribute to their health, and I explain that it is often a cumulative effect that triggers health problems. In most cases, it is not our last meal that makes us ill, but our last thousand meals. Allergy sufferers are painfully aware of how eating the wrong foods can affect their health but we all need to remember that the right food is a medicine and that a balanced, varied diet is one of the simplest ways to better health.

To survive, the human body needs many factors, including vitamins, minerals, amino acids, essential fatty acids, plus air, water, and light. Our bodies cannot manufacture these factors, we must take them from external sources. To obtain adequate nutrients essential for health, our diet needs to contain sufficient quantities of high quality, fresh, unrefined wholefoods as possible. Because many fruits and vegetables are flown thousands of miles to reach our table and, once harvested, can lose up to 50 percent of their vitamin content in just 10 days, we recommend that you eat locally grown, seasonal, and preferably organic, foods whenever possible.

Our health depends not only on what we eat, but also on our body's ability to absorb nutrients within the gut. Many people over forty have digestive problems, often induced by stress and over-consumption of junk foods eaten in a hurry. One secret to improving absorption is to chew food more thoroughly, and to eat a little fresh pineapple or papaya, which contain digestive enzymes, with main meals or you can take a digestive enzyme tablet—these are available from all good health food stores.

Vitamins, minerals, and essential fats from our food work synergistically (together) within the body, so you derive greater benefits from eating a variety of wholefoods, rather than taking vitamin pills in isolation. An alfalfa sprout sandwich, for example, contains more nutrients than a cheap multi-vitamin tablet. Our bodies consist of approximately 63 percent water, 22 percent protein, 13 percent fat, and 2 percent vitamins and minerals and for optimum health we need to eat a balance of all the main food types— carbohydrates, proteins, and fats.

For energy, the body prefers unrefined carbohydrates that release their natural sugars more slowly than highly refined foods such as mass-produced cakes and cookies. For optimum health, 60 to 70 percent of your diet should consist of unrefined, fiber-rich carbohydrates, which will help to raise your energy levels and encourage the elimination of toxins. These carbohydrates include whole grains, such as brown rice, millet, rye, unrefined whole-wheat cereals, breads, pasta, or legumes, and wholefoods, such as vegetables and fruits. Sugar is a carbohydrate, but after giving an initial energy burst, it can actually drain energy levels. We have suggested a few healthier alternatives, but they still contain sugar and should be used in moderation. It is worth noting that the foods you crave most such as saturated fats, sugar, and alcohol, are often contributory factors to many health problems. Also, many foods labelled "low fat" in fact have a high sugar content, and sugar in excess converts to fat in the body if it is not burned up during exercise. So read labels carefully!

Proteins are essential for muscle tone and growth, healthy skin and nails, for tissue repair, and in the manufacture of hormones. They should make up 15 to 20 percent of your daily diet. Vegetable-based proteins such as lentils, kidney beans, soybean curd, navy beans, peas, corn, broccoli, runner beans, and nuts (Brazil, almonds, walnuts, and pecan nuts are proteins), are preferable to animal-based proteins, as they are low in saturated (hard) fats and high in fiber. But again, as balance and variety are important, if you are not a vegetarian you can also enjoy fresh fish, free-range eggs and chicken, and a little meat (preferably organic).

There is a great deal of misunderstanding regarding fats; many people believe that low-fat or no-fat diets are more healthy, but they are mistaken. We all need a certain amount of fat, but it is the type of fat that is important. There are two kinds of fats: saturated and unsaturated. Saturated fats are the unhealthier fats, found mainly in meat and dairy products, and these are linked to hardening of the arteries and most major diseases. Unsaturated fats are the healthier fats, found in nuts, seeds, and oily fish. Unsaturated fats fall into two types: monounsaturated fats are found in olive oil and avocados; polyunsaturated fats are found in nuts and seeds. For optimum health, a sufficient intake of certain fats known as essential fats are needed by every cell in the body to function properly. A lack of essential fats is linked to dry skin, eczema, psoriasis, water retention, hyperactivity, mood swings, and an inability to lose weight. Essential fats are found in seeds such as sunflower, sesame, pumpkin, and linseeds, and in their unrefined oils, and also in oily fish. Essential fats are easily destroyed when heated and by exposure to oxygen, so store salad dressings in the refrigerator. Many processed foods, such as cakes, pies, sausages, margarines, and burgers, contain "hydrogenated" or "trans-fats," which should be avoided as much as possible. Although butter is a saturated fat, Kathryn and I prefer butter when baking, because it does not turn rancid when heated and is rich in vitamin A. Fats, mainly in the form of essential fats, should make up no more than 30 percent of your daily diet.

Try to eat eat five types of fruits and vegetables, which are packed with nutrients and fiber, every day. Drink plenty of water, avoid excessive use of salt, and do some exercise every day. If we all did this, there would be a substantial decrease in heart disease, high blood pressure, and degenerative conditions—even in the most ardent carnivores.

Remember that your body is capable of healing itself when given the right tools for the job. Every 72 hours your gut lining is completely replaced; every month your skin is renewed, every two years you manufacture a new skeleton and a new liver. The body strives to maintain a healthy balance, and our aim in this book is to help you to discover that balance through a great variety of delicious recipes.

Fresh vegetables and whole grains are packed with nutrients that will improve your looks and boost your energy level.

what are body *and* beauty foods *and* how do they work?

THE OLD SAYING *"you are what you eat" is absolutely right. Food has the power to heal, energize, and make us look more beautiful. The properties of certain foods have been known for generations, and modern science has uncovered the reasons why many tried and trusted recipes work. Research has* also shown *which other foods can positively enhance health, vitality and appearance. By choosing meals carefully, we can give our bodies a boost every day. All the foods listed here as well as the delicious recipes that follow are packed with nutritional gems. Read on and discover the best body and beauty foods!*

Fruit

apples

● Apples protect the heart. They are recommended for anyone with high blood cholesterol or blood glucose problems, such as hypoglycemia or diabetes. Grated or mashed apple is an old remedy for diarrhea. For weight watchers, apples are good to eat just before meals, as they blunt the appetite, and, as a between-meal snack.

● Fiber. A medium apple provides 15% of the daily recommendation for fiber. Some of this is soluble fiber, which may help lower blood cholesterol.

● Pectin. Apples are rich in the soluble fiber pectin. Eating two apples a day pushes enough pectin through the blood to make a real dent in cholesterol levels for some people.

● Rich in vitamin C, plus worthwhile amounts of vitamin E.

apricots

● Flavonoids. Apricots contain flavonoids which strengthen capillaries, reducing the risk of bleeding and bruising.

● Beta carotene. Good for eyes, bones, and teeth, and boosting immune function.

● Vitamin C. Used in the manufacture of collagen, the "glue" that gives skin its elasticity and support, vital for wound healing and protection against infection. Common signs of deficiency are bleeding gums, thread veins, and slow wound healing.

bananas

● Pectin. Bananas have a higher pectin content even than apples. They are sweet, filling, sustaining, and easy on the digestion. Bananas are a good food for anyone who suffers from acid indigestion, reflux, or ulcers, and are a good "settling" food after a stomach upset. Super-gentle fiber.

● Magnesium. Works with essential fatty acids, calcium, and the B-complex group to support the nervous system and maintain healthy cell production.

● Vitamin C, folic acid, vitamin B$_6$, pectin, potassium.

blackberries

● Calcium and magnesium. Blackberries are especially rich in these, so are a good food for the bones.

● Vitamin C. A cup of blackberries provides half the recommended daily intake.

blackcurrants

● Antioxidants and B-group vitamins, essential to eye health.

● Flavonoids. Often found in the same foods that contain vitamin C.

● Fiber.

● Vitamin C. One half cup of blackcurrants provides more than 100% of the daily recommendation for vitamin C.

blueberries

● Antioxidants and B group vitamins. Antioxidants are essential to eye health.

● Vitamin C.

cantaloupe and other melons

● A rich source of carotenoids, which are excellent antioxidants (particularly cantaloupe melon).

● Flavonoids.

carambolas (star fruit)

● Great eaten straight, like apples, or sliced into fruit salads, blended into fresh fruit juices, or used as a garnish for salads and cheeseboards.

● Top ratings for vitamin C.

cherries

● Beta carotene—vital for bones and teeth.

● Vitamin C.

figs

- One of the "super-foods." Fresh figs are delicious in fruit salads. Sweet-tasting, dried figs make great alternatives to candies and chocolate. They are wonderful chopped into breakfast cereals or eaten as a snack with nuts, seeds, and other dried fruit.
- Calcium. Good for the bones.
- Fiber. Packed with dietary fiber, so very valuable for bowel health.
- Magnesium.

grapefruit

- Citrus fruits are a rich source of vitamin C and potassium. Pink and red varieties are high in beta carotene.
- Flavonoids. Often found in the same foods that contain vitamin C. Flavonoids strengthen capillaries, reducing the risk of bleeding and bruising. Deficiency signs are similar to those of vitamin C. Best source: pith and zest of the fruit.

grapes

- Good source of antioxidants, particularly resveratrol, which scientists believe has anti-cancer and cholesterol-lowering properties.

kiwi fruit

- A very fine source of vitamin C—weight for weight, more than twice that of oranges. One kiwi provides more than 100% of the daily recommendation for vitamin C.
- Calcium and magnesium. Good for the bones.
- Fiber.
- Small amounts of iron and B vitamins.

lemons

- Lemons have a reputation as a skin food; dabbing fresh lemon juice on to the skin, and massaging it in with a some virgin olive oil, is an old remedy for improving skin condition and reducing wrinkles.
- Flavonoids.
- Vitamin C.

limes

- An excellent source of vitamin C—4 fluid ounces of lime juice provides 30mg, about half the adult daily requirement.

mangoes

- Good source of carotenoids, which are excellent antioxidants.
- Vitamin C.
- Vitamin E.
- Niacin.
- Potassium.

nectarines

- Good source of carotenoids, which are excellent antioxidants.
- Vitamin C. Make a super-C juice by blending nectarines with kiwi fruit, a squeeze of fresh lemon, and honey.

oranges

- One medium-sized orange provides more than the adult daily requirement of vitamin C.
- Folate, thiamine, potassium.

papayas (papaw)

- Papayas contain papain, an enzyme that is similar to the digestive juice pepsin, so is good eaten after a meal.
- Flavonoids.
- Good source of carotenoids, which are excellent antioxidants.
- Vitamin C.

peaches

- Good source of carotenoids, which are excellent antioxidants.

pineapples

- Vitamin C. Choose fresh ones where possible, canning can destroy some of the vitamin C content. One of the few fruits (papaya and papaw are others) that is best eaten directly after a meal because it contains natural digestive enzymes that help to break down other food. Always swill the mouth and teeth with water after eating pineapple. It can erode tooth enamel very easily.

raspberries

- B group vitamins and antioxidants that are essential to eye health.
- Good source of carotenoids, which are excellent antioxidants.
- Vitamin C.

strawberries

- B group vitamins and antioxidants that are essential to eye health.
- Good source of carotenoids, which are excellent antioxidants.
- Vitamin C.

Dried fruit

- Figs, yellow apricots, Hunza apricots, golden raisins, raisins, prunes, and dates are great treats for anyone with a sweet tooth. Renowned for their gentle dietary fiber, dried fruits are also packed with beta carotene and potassium. Hunzas (available from most health food stores) are not so well known, but are the tastiest and most nourishing of all apricots. Many dried fruits are treated with sulfite preservatives, which may present a problem for asthmatics.
- Boron. This is still a little-known trace element, needed in small amounts, but essential for healthy bones and teeth. It may be of particular importance in the prevention of osteoporosis and arthritis so it is good for the joints.
- Magnesium. Works with essential fatty acids, calcium, and the B group of vitamins to maintain healthy cell production and bones, and support the nervous system and heart.

Vegetables

artichokes

- A natural diuretic and good for the digestion. Contains cyanarin, which is believed to protect the liver.
- Beta carotene, folic acid, most minerals.

asparagus

- Chock-full of antioxidants, vitamin C, carotene, and folic acid. An excellent diuretic that helps rid the body of salt and excess water.
- Chromium. An important factor in balancing blood glucose and blood fats, and in protecting the nervous system.
- Beta carotene. Good for the eyes and immune function.
- Vitamin E. Prolongs cell life, hastens wound healing, and helps to reduce scarring. Research suggests that vitamin E may be more effective when taken with other antioxidants, especially selenium and vitamins A and C. Easy bruising and dry skin are common signs of deficiency.

avocado

- Avocados are an excellent skin food, both eaten and applied to the skin. Sadly avoided by many people because they are seen as a high-calorie, fattening food, avocados should be classed with the "healthy fats" and included more often in the diet.
- Monounsaturates (as in olive oil) and vitamin E.

bamboo shoots

- Contain trace amounts of vitamin C, calcium, and iron.
- Potassium.

beans, green

- Fiber.
- Vitamin C.

beets

- Washed, peeled and mixed with a handful of grapes, an apple, and a couple of carrots, this makes the most delicious fruit-flavored and beautifully colored red juice.
- Chromium. An important factor in balancing blood glucose and blood fats, and in protecting the nervous system.
- Fabulous for folate, vitamin C, carotenoids, and potassium.

bell peppers

- Rich in vitamin C. Used in the manufacture of collagen, the "glue" that gives skin its elasticity and support. Vital for wound healing and protecting against infection.

brassicas

- The brassicas are an important immune-boosting group that includes Brussels sprouts, all kinds of cabbage including pak choy and red cabbage, Chinese broccoli, green and purple broccoli/calabrese, cauliflower, kale. Brassicas are good bone-boosting foods. The stalks, unless too tough to use, should always be sliced up and included in the cooking as they are a rich source of minerals. Kale and Chinese broccoli are especially high in calcium.
- Vitamin C. Good for the immune system. Some vitamin E, a few B vitamins, folic acid.
- Sulforaphane, calcium, magnesium, silica, iron. Sulforaphane is another important anti-cancer chemical.
- Plenty of dietary fiber.

broccoli

- Broccoli stalks are particularly rich in calcium. Tiny raw florets used in salads will raise the meal's vitamin C content.
- Flavonoids.
- High scores for sulforaphane, beta carotene, folate, potassium, magnesium, calcium.

carrots

- Contain varying amounts of dietary fiber, beta carotene, and phenols (sometimes listed as polyphenols)—powerful antioxidant substances that scientists believe may also have immune-boosting properties.
- Abundant in carotenoids, which include beta carotene. Five to six servings of these brightly colored foods each day could reduce significantly the risk of cancer and heart disease, and could mean catching fewer viruses.
- Beta carotene. Vital for bones, teeth, eyes, and immune function. Juicing increases the bio-availability of the carotene. Helps support the eyes and boost the immune system.
- Carrots also contain small amounts of calcium.

celery

- Great in salads and juiced with other vegetables such as carrot and watercress, and sweetened with apple.
- Vitamin C. A cup of chopped celery provides 10% of the daily recommendation for vitamin C.

dandelion leaves

- Freshly picked young leaves can give a nutritious boost to salads. Dandelion is naturally diuretic.

garlic

- Modern science has now confirmed that garlic taken regularly reduces cholesterol levels and blood viscosity and boosts immunity—garlic has antibacterial properties. Alliums may also block the formation of carcinogenic compounds.
- Garlic and onions may reduce the risk of thrombosis and hypertension.
- Garlic might help in the treatment of nasal congestion.
- Raw garlic is more effective than cooked, and the odor is less strong if used regularly. Those who cannot tolerate garlic (it can cause indigestion in some people) might consider garlic capsules.

- Selenium. Trace element is now recognized as a vital antioxidant, being important not only for a strong immune system, but also for a healthy heart and circulation, and the joints.

ginger, fresh root

- When used as a seasoning, fresh ginger contributes trace amounts of minerals.

green vegetables, leafy

- Because of their antioxidant capabilities, leafy green vegetables are also important foods for eye protection, including reducing the risk of cataracts and an age-related eye condition known as macular degeneration.
- Boron. A little-known trace element needed in small amounts, but essential for healthy bones and teeth. It may be of particular importance in the prevention of osteoporosis and arthritis. Good for the joints. Like selenium, however, boron levels in food will depend on soil status.
- Calcium. For healthy blood, blood vessels, skin, bones, and muscle tissue. Calcium works with vitamin C in collagen production. Those all-important essential fatty acids won't be properly utilized without calcium. Apart from weakened bones, too little calcium has a detrimental effect upon the nervous system.
- Magnesium. Works with essential fatty acids, calcium, and the B-complex group to support the nervous system and maintain healthy cell production.
- Selenium. Antioxidant and anti-inflammatory, it supports the immune function and improves resistance to infection. Essential for healthy skin, nails, and hair.
- The B complex group of vitamins for the repair and regeneration of skin tissue, to support the nervous system, and for deriving energy from food—thiamin (B_1), riboflavin (B_2), niacin (B_3), pantothenic acid (B_5), pyridoxine (B_6), cyanocobalamin (B_{12}), folic acid, biotin. Deficiency signs include sensitive skin, "tingling" sensations in the limbs, cracks, or sores, especially around the mouth and nose, and itchy, inflamed eyes.

- Vitamin C. Used in the manufacture of collagen, the "glue" that gives skin its elasticity and support. Vital for wound healing and protecting against infection.
- Vitamin E. Vitamin E prolongs cell life, hastens wound healing, and helps reduce scarring. A vital antioxidant. Research suggests that vitamin E may be more effective when taken with other antioxidants, especially selenium and vitamins A and C.

onions

- Selenium. Trace element is now recognized as a vital antioxidant, essential for healthy skin, nails, and hair. Flaking or bleeding nails, poor wound healing, dull, dry hair, and dry skin can indicate selenium deficiency.

parsley

- Parsley is a natural diuretic and digestive aid. All culinary herbs are rich in nutrients. Including them in salads and cooking is a good way to add extra vitamins and minerals.
- An abundance of potassium, folic acid, and carotene.
- Iron. Essential for healthy blood. Pale, brittle nails and pale skin may be indications of iron deficiency.
- Beta carotene. Good for the eyes and immune function.
- Vitamin C.

potatoes

- Vitamin C.
- Vitamins B_3 and B_6.

pumpkin

- Beta carotene. Good for the eyes and immune function.

root vegetables

- Fiber.
- Folic acid and vitamin C.
- Selenium. Antioxidant, anti-inflammatory, supports immune function and improves resistance to infection, essential for healthy skin, nails, and hair.

▌ **spinach**

● Because of its antioxidant capabilities, spinach is important for eye protection, including reducing the risk of cataracts and an age-related eye condition known as macular degeneration.

● Magnesium, carotene, and folic acid. Magnesium is an essential heart nutrient as well as being good for the teeth and bones.

● Beta carotene. Good for the eyes and immune function.

▌ **squash, winter**

● Excellent source of carotenoids.

▌ **sweet potatoes**

● Not, in fact, a potato at all, but related to the yam family. Red flesh sweet potatoes are loaded with potassium.

● Beta carotene. Good for the eyes and immune function.

▌ **tomatoes**

● Tomatoes are worth a special mention because they are particularly rich in vitamin C and lycopene, also some dietary fiber. Tomatoes belong to the deadly nightshade family and were once thought to be poisonous. Blamed by some for aggravating arthritis and food allergies, tomatoes have more recently been hailed as an anti-cancer food. Worth including in the diet several times each week. Lycopene (a carotene) is released when tomatoes are cooked, and better absorbed when eaten with a little oil.

● Selenium.

▌ **watercress**

● Beta carotene.
● Vitamin C.

Fish

▌ **fresh fish**

● Magnesium. Magnesium-rich foods are just as important for maintaining healthy muscles, bones, and teeth as calcium. It is an absolutely essential heart nutrient.

● Selenium. Vital antioxidant, being important not only for a strong immune system, but also for a healthy heart and circulation, and joints. Anti-inflammatory, improves resistance to infection, essential for healthy skin, nails, and hair.

▌ **oily fish**

● Oily fish—especially mackerel, salmon, pilchards, tuna, and trout—are rich in omega-3 essential fatty acids. These are vital for healthy heart function and circulation and they reduce the stickiness of the blood and help to improve the ratio of good cholesterol (high-density lipoprotein—HDL). Essential fatty acids are vital for every cell in the body to function properly.

▌ **salmon**

● Vitamins A and D.
● Vitamins B_1, B_2, B_3, B_5, B_6, B_{12}, and biotin.

● Calcium (canned salmon only) and magnesium are essential heart nutrients as well as being good for the teeth and bones. For healthy blood, blood vessels, skin, bones, and muscle tissue. Calcium works with vitamin C in collagen production. Those all-important essential fatty acids won't be properly utilized without calcium.

● Omega-3 group of essential fatty acids. Essential fatty acids are important for healthy sight.

▌ **mackerel**

● Calcium (canned mackerel only) and magnesium. Essential heart nutrients as well as being good for the teeth and bones. For healthy blood, blood vessels, skin, bones, and muscle tissue. Calcium works with vitamin C in collagen production..

Those all-important essential fatty acids won't be properly utilized without calcium.

● Zinc. (canned mackerel only). Immune-boosting and essential for healthy skin.

● Omega-3 group of essential fatty acids. Essential fatty acids are important for healthy sight.

▌ **seafood (shellfish)**

● Chromium. An important factor in balancing blood glucose and blood fats, and in protecting the nervous system.

● Selenium.

● Zinc. For wound healing, healthy growth and repair of cells. Excessively oily or very dry skin, persistent infections, white marks on fingernails, and slow wound healing are signs of zinc deficiency.

Meat

▌ **lamb**

● Magnesium. Magnesium-rich foods are just as important as calcium for maintaining healthy muscles, bones, and teeth. It is an absolutely essential heart nutrient.

● B vitamins.
● Iron.
● Zinc.

▌ **chicken liver**

● The B-complex group—for the repair and regeneration of skin tissue, to support the nervous system and for release of energy from food. Includes thiamin (B_1), riboflavin (B_2), niacin (B_3), pantothenic acid (B_5), pyridoxine (B_6), cyanocobalamin (B_{12}), folic acid, biotin. Deficiency signs include sensitive skin, "tingling" sensations in the limbs, cracks, or sores, especially around the mouth and nose, and itchy, inflamed eyes.

• Chromium. An important factor in balancing blood glucose and blood fats, and in protecting the nervous system.

● Vitamin A. Liver is one of the highest providers of retinol.

● Iron.
● Selenium.

▌ **poultry**

● Protein.
● B vitamins.
● Zinc. Immune-boosting and essential for maintaining healthy skin.

▌ **stock (made with bones)**

● Calcium. An essential heart nutrient as well as being good for the teeth and bones.

Cereals

▌ **millet**

● Zinc. For wound healing, healthy growth and repair of cells. Excessively oily or very dry skin, persistent infections, white marks on fingernails, and slow wound healing are all signs of zinc deficiency.

▌ **oats**

● Good source of soluble fiber, which may help reduce cholesterol.

● Vitamin B_1.

● Small amounts of vitamins B_2, B_3, B_6, and folic acid.

● Zinc. For wound healing, healthy growth and repair of cells. Excessively oily or very dry skin, persistent infections, white marks on fingernails, and slow wound healing are all signs of zinc deficiency.

▌ **pasta**

● Protein.
● Vitamins B_1, B_3. ·
● Iron.
● Small amounts of magnesium, phosphorus, and zinc.

rice (brown)

- Essential fatty acids.
- Magnesium. As important as calcium for maintaining healthy muscles, bones, and teeth.
- Selenium.
- Zinc.
- Many times more nourishing than white rice, brown rice is also an excellent source of potassium, vitamin B_3, vitamin E, and folic acid—and, of course, gentle but effective dietary fiber.

rye

- Zinc. For wound healing, healthy growth and repair of cells. Excessively oily or very dry skin, persistent infections, white marks on fingernails, and slow wound healing are all signs of zinc deficiency.

whole grains

- The B-complex group
- Chromium.
- Magnesium.
- Selenium.
- Vitamin E.

Beans and legumes

- The B-complex group (for the repair and regeneration of skin tissue, to support the nervous system, and release of energy from food)—thiamin (B_1), riboflavin (B_2), niacin (B_3), pantothenic acid (B_5), pyridoxine (B_6), cyanocobalamin (B_{12}), folic acid, biotin. Deficiency signs include sensitive skin, "tingling" sensations in the limbs, cracks or sores, especially around the mouth and nose, and itchy, inflamed eyes.
- Iron. Essential for healthy blood. Pale, brittle nails and pale skin may be indications of iron deficiency.
- Magnesium. Magnesium-rich foods, such as legumes, are just as important for maintaining healthy muscles, bones, and

teeth as calcium. It is an absolutely essential heart nutrient. Works with essential fatty acids, calcium, and the B-complex group to support the nervous system and maintain healthy cell production.
- Vitamin B_2. Deficiency symptoms can include conjunctivitis, bloodshot eyes, and cataracts.
- Zinc. Immune-boosting essential.

garbanzo beans

- Zinc. Immune-boosting and essential for maintaining healthy skin.

lentils

- Zinc. Immune-boosting and essential for maintaining healthy skin.

peas

- Vitamin C.
- Folic acid.
- Fiber.
- Small amounts of iron, zinc, and magnesium.

red kidney beans

- Zinc. Boosts immune function and essential for maintaining healthy skin.

soybeans

- Calcium. For healthy blood, blood vessels, skin, bones, and muscle tissue. Those all-important essential fatty acids won't be properly utilized without calcium. Soybeans are thought by some people to help balance hormones.
- Good source of phytoestrogens which may help reduce the risk of breast and prostate cancer.
- Tofu (bean curd)—an excellent protein source for vegetarians, rich in calcium, magnesium, iron, and some vitamin E.

Dairy products

butter

- Vitamin A. Good for the eyes. To avoid too much fat in your diet, use in moderation.

buttermilk

- Calcium.

cheese

- Calcium.
- Vitamin A. Good for the eyes.
- Vitamin B_2. Deficiency symptoms can include conjunctivitis, bloodshot eyes, and cataracts.
- Zinc. For wound healing, healthy growth, and repair of cells. Excessively oily or very dry skin, persistent infections, white marks on fingernails, and slow wound healing are all signs of zinc deficiency.
- Use in moderation and choose low-fat cheeses as much as possible.

eggs

- Protein.
- Chromium. An important factor in balancing blood glucose and blood fats, and in protecting the nervous system.
- Selenium and small amounts of iron and zinc.
- Vitamin A. Good for the eyes.
- Vitamin B_2. Deficiency symptoms can include conjunctivitis, bloodshot eyes, and cataracts.
- Eggs provide some vitamins B_3, B_{12}, D, E, and folic acid.

yogurt

- Calcium.
- Yogurt with live and active cultures is beneficial not only to the digestion but also to the gut generally, being a valuable source of friendly bacteria. Topically, live yogurt can be used to soothe mild sunburn, as a face pack, and to treat vaginal and oral thrush.
- Yogurt provides easily digestible

protein, magnesium, potassium, zinc, vitamins B_1 and B_2, and vitamin A.
- Vitamin B_2. Deficiency symptoms can include conjunctivitis, bloodshot eyes, and cataracts.

Nuts

- All contain potassium, magnesium, selenium, iron and zinc. They are valuable also for their dietary fiber and the monounsaturated and polyunsaturated fatty acid content. For best nourishment value, nuts should be purchased fresh and unbroken, not salted, crushed or roasted.
- The B-complex group. For the repair and regeneration of skin tissue, to support the nervous system, and for the release of energy from food.
- Calcium. For healthy blood, blood vessels, skin, bones and muscle tissue. Calcium works with vitamin C in collagen production.
- Iron. Essential for healthy blood. Pale, brittle nails and pale skin may be indications of iron deficiency.
- Zinc. For wound healing, healthy growth, and repair of cells. Excessively oily or very dry skin, persistent infections, white marks on fingernails. and slow wound healing are all signs of zinc deficiency.

almonds

- Calcium.
- Magnesium.
- Omega-6 essential fatty acids.
- Potassium, selenium, iron, and zinc.

Brazil nuts

- Calcium.
- Magnesium.
- Omega-6 essential fatty acids.
- Potassium, selenium, iron, and zinc.
- Valuable also for their dietary fiber and monounsaturated and polyunsaturated fatty acid content.

cashew nuts

- Magnesium.

hazelnuts

- Boron.
- Potassium, magnesium, iron, and zinc.
- Valuable also for their dietary fiber and monounsaturated and polyunsaturated fatty acid content.

macadamia nuts

- Potassium and iron.
- Valuable also for their dietary fiber and monounsaturated and polyunsaturated fatty acid content.

walnuts

- Omega-3 essential fatty acids.

Seeds

- Edible seeds include pumpkin, sesame, sunflower, linseeds, poppy, celery, dill, fennel, fenugreek. Rich in essential fatty acids. Seeds are providers of zinc, potassium, magnesium, and iron. Sunflower seeds are especially good for vitamin E. Sesame seeds are high in calcium.
- The B-complex group—for the repair and regeneration of skin tissue, to support the nervous system, and for release of energy from food—thiamin (B_1), riboflavin (B_2), niacin (B_3), pantothenic acid (B_5), pyridoxine (B_6), cyanocobalamin (B_{12}), folic acid, biotin. Deficiency signs include sensitive skin, "tingling" sensations in the limbs, cracks, or sores, especially around the mouth and nose, and itchy, inflamed eyes.
- Calcium. For healthy blood, blood vessels, skin, bones, and muscle tissue. Calcium works with vitamin C in collagen production. Those all-important essential fatty acids won't be properly utilized without calcium. Apart from weakened bones, too little calcium has a detrimental effect upon the nervous system.
- Iron. Essential for healthy blood. Pale, brittle nails and pale skin may be indications of iron deficiency.

- Vitamin E. Prolongs cell life, hastens wound healing and helps reduce scarring. A vital antioxidant. Research suggests that vitamin E may be more effective when taken with other antioxidants, especially selenium and vitamins A and C. Easy bruising and dry skin are common signs of deficiency.
- Zinc. For wound healing, healthy growth, and repair of cells.

linseeds and flaxseeds

- Rich in essential fatty acids. Contain zinc, potassium, magnesium, and iron.

pumpkin seeds

- Contain essential fatty acids, potassium, magnesium, and iron.
- Zinc. Immune-boosting essential.

sesame seeds

- Calcium. For healthy blood, blood vessels, skin, bones, and muscle tissue. Calcium works with vitamin C in collagen production. Those all-important essential fatty acids won't be properly utilized without calcium.
- Vitamin E. Prolongs cell life, hastens wound healing and helps reduce scarring. A vital antioxidant.
- Rich in essential fatty acids. Contain small amounts of magnesium, phosphorus, and iron.
- Tahini. Similar profile to sesame seeds.

sunflower seeds

- Rich in essential fatty acids. Also high in zinc, potassium, magnesium, vitamins B_3 and B_6, and folic acid.
- Sunflower seeds are especially good for vitamin E.

Oils

almond oil

- Omega-6 essential fatty acids.

cold-pressed oils

- Cold-pressed oils are those such as sunflower, sesame, walnut, extra virgin olive oil, safflower, soybean, and linseed oil. Most mass-produced cooking oils are processed and refined using heat and solvents. Cold-pressing is a more expensive method, but retains more of the natural goodness of the oil, in particular the substances known as essential fatty acids or EFAs. As polyunsaturated oils tend to be less stable when heated, it's best to keep them for salads and light cooking. Extra virgin olive oil is predominantly monounsaturated and more stable at higher temperatures, although frying will impair the flavor. Try to include a tablespoon of some kind of cold-pressed, unrefined oil in the diet every day and keep these oils in the refrigerator so that they retain their freshness.
- Vitamin E. Hastens wound healing and helps reduce scarring.

fish oils

- Rich in omega-3 essential fatty acids, which are found in every single cell structure in the body and are vital for good muscle tone, healthy hair, strong nails, hormone production, and healthy skin. Weak, flaking nails, dry hair, and flaking skin are common signs of deficiency.
- Vitamin A-rich fish oils, such as cod liver oil, are excellent for eyes, help to protect cell membranes and may reduce the risk of glaucoma.
- Vitamin D.

olive oil (extra virgin)

- Rich in monounsaturates. The best choice of oil for cooking; although frying impairs its flavor. It also makes delicious salad dressings.

Sugars

blackstrap molasses

- Iron. Essential for healthy blood. Pale, brittle nails, pale skin, and constant lethargy may be indications of iron deficiency.
- Calcium.
- Magnesium.

honey

- Ordinary honey has about the same nutritional profile as sugar. Health food advocates maintain that best-quality, cold-pressed raw honey is usually single source (not blended), nearly always organic, and usually produced without the need to feed bees on sugar. Like all sugars, honey should be used in moderation.

notes *on* ingredients

Whenever possible, use fresh vegetables, fruit, and juices. Organically grown produce is preferable as it is free from chemical fertilizers. Cooking vegetables by steaming or microwaving is the best way to retain their nutrients.

Organic dairy products—milk, butter, cheese, and yogurt—are available in health food stores and major supermarkets. People who are allergic to or intolerant of cow's milk can use goat's milk, and sheep's or goat's milk yogurt. Although no significant nutritional difference between organic and intensively farmed produce has yet been proved, you may prefer to use free-range lamb, poultry, and eggs.

Oils such as sunflower, sesame, hazelnut, and walnut should be cold-pressed. Most mass-produced cooking oils are processed using heat and solvents. Cold-pressing is a more expensive method, but retains more of the natural goodness of the oil, in particular the essential fatty acids (EFAs) and vitamin E. When a recipe includes olive oil, the best kind to use is extra virgin olive oil. Because it is produced by pressure, rather than by chemical processing, the antioxidants are preserved to give better nutritional value and flavor.

The use of white sugar should be kept to a minimum. Organic cane sugar, molasses, real maple syrup, and cold-pressed honey are alternatives that also should be used in moderation.

Whole grains such as brown rice, oats, rye, millet, barley, and couscous are excellent sources of fiber and vitamins of the B-complex. If bread is to be served with a meal should be of the organic whole-wheat variety. For people with gluten sensitivity, gluten-free flours and pasta, made from potato, rice, buckwheat, or legumes, are available.

Soy sauce contains some useful minerals, but these include high levels of sodium. Being careful of your salt intake is important if you have high blood pressure. None of the recipes include more than a tablespoon of soy sauce, but some people may prefer to use the reduced-salt version.

notes *on the* recipes

 Spoon measurements used in this book are metric:

1 teaspoon = *5 ml*
1 tablespoon = *15 ml*

The preparation and cooking times are approximate. Ovens and broilers should be preheated to the temperature that is specified in the recipe. The cooking times for all the recipes in this book are based on the oven or broiler being preheated. If using a fan oven, follow the manufacturer's directions for adjusting the time and temperature.

Frozen dishes may be defrosted in the microwave, or left for several hours or overnight in the refrigerator.

Fresh herbs are used in many of the recipes. Fresh herbs give a better flavor, but if dried herbs are used instead of fresh, one tablespoon of fresh herbs is equivalent to one teaspoon of dried herbs. This does not apply to recipes where dried herbs only are listed, such as dried *herbes de provence*, a mixture of rosemary, thyme, sage, parsley and bay leaves.

basic recipes

homemade chicken stock

■ ingredients

- free-range chicken bones—fresh or the carcass from cooked meat
- 1 onion or 2 leeks, sliced
- 2 carrots, sliced
- 2 celery stalks, chopped
- 1 bay leaf or 1 fresh bouquet garni

makes approx
3 cups / 1¼ pints (700ml)

■ method

1 Break or chop the chicken carcass into pieces and place in a large saucepan.
2 Add the prepared vegetables and bay leaf or bouquet garni with 3½ pints (1.7 liters) cold water.
3 Bring to a boil; then reduce the heat, partially cover the pan, and simmer gently for about 2 hours. Skim off and discard any scum and fat.
4 Strain the stock through a sieve. When cold, remove and discard all the fat. Cool slightly, then refrigerate for up to 3 days.
5 When required for use, season to taste with sea salt and freshly ground black pepper.

homemade vegetable stock

■ ingredients

- 2 onions, sliced
- 1 large carrot, sliced
- 1 leek, sliced
- 4 celery stalks, chopped
- 1 small turnip or 4 ounces (115g) rutabaga, diced
- 1 parsnip, sliced
- 1 fresh bouquet garni or 1 bay leaf

makes approx
6 cups / 2¼ pints (1.3 liters)

■ method

1 Put the prepared vegetables and bouquet garni or bay leaf in a large saucepan. Then add 3½ pints (1.7 liters) cold water.
2 Bring to a boil; then reduce the heat, partially cover the pan, and simmer gently for 1–1½ hours. Skim off and discard any scum that rises to the surface during cooking.
3 Strain the stock through a sieve.
4 Season to taste with sea salt and freshly ground black pepper.

If not required immediately, this stock can be kept in the refrigerator in a covered container for up to 3 days, or frozen for up to 3 months.

mayonnaise

■ ingredients

- 2 egg yolks
- 2tbsp vinegar or lemon juice
- 2tbsp water
- 1tsp sugar
- 1tsp dry mustard
- ½tsp salt
- dash of pepper
- 1 cup of cooking oil

makes approx
1¼ cups/7 fluid ounces (200ml)

■ method

1 In a small saucepan, stir together the egg yolks, vinegar, water, sugar, mustard, salt and pepper until thoroughly blended. Cook over very low heat, stirring constantly, until mixture bubbles in 1 or 2 places. Remove from heat. Let stand for 4 minutes.
2 Pour into blender container. Cover and blend at high speed. While blending, very slowly add oil. Blend until thick and smooth. Occasionally, turn off blender and scrape down sides of container with rubber spatula, if necessary. Cover and refrigerate if not using immediately. Use homemade mayonnaise within 5 days.

french dressing

■ ingredients

- 6tbsp olive oil
- 2tbsp white wine or cider vinegar, or lemon juice
- 1–2tsp Dijon mustard
- dash of sugar
- 1 small clove garlic, crushed
- 1–2tbsp chopped fresh mixed herbs
- sea salt
- freshly ground black pepper

makes approx
⅔ cup/¼ pint (150ml)

■ method

1 Put all the ingredients in a small bowl and whisk together until thoroughly mixed. Alternatively, place all the ingredients in a clean, screw-top jar, seal, and shake well until thoroughly mixed.
2 Adjust the seasoning and serve immediately or keep in a screw-top jar in the refrigerator for up to 1 week. Shake thoroughly before serving.

body

In this section you will find recipes containing foods to help boost your immune system, encourage strong teeth and bone growth, support the health of your heart and circulatory system, and to help keep joints flexible. Your immune system needs vitamins A and C, plus the minerals zinc and selenium, in order to stay healthy. Oily fish and liver are rich in vitamin A; sweet potatoes and carrots are all rich in beta carotene, which the body can convert into vitamin A. For zinc and selenium, which are also good for the heart, eat shellfish, meat, poultry, split peas, pumpkin seeds, lentils, brown rice, garlic, Brazil nuts, raw wheatgerm, and other grains. Vitamin C is an overall star when it comes to health, but especially rich sources include oranges, grape-fruits, kiwi fruits, lemons, limes, red bell peppers, kale, tomatoes, broccoli, and Brussels sprouts. Most fruits and vegetables supply some vitamin C.

FOODS

A healthy heart and good circulation require that the body gets adequate magnesium, selenium, calcium, vitamin E, and omega-3 and -6 essential fatty acids. Oily fish is rich in omega-3 essentials fats, which reduce the risk of blood clots and lower low-density lipoprotein (LDL)—the type of cholesterol that can lead to heart disease. Walnuts, linseeds, sunflower and pumpkin seeds, and their oils, are rich in both omega-3 and -6 fatty acids and also contain vitamin E, which helps to protect the heart and joints. Avocados, wheat germ, and leafy green vegetables such as broccoli are all rich in vitamin E. For calcium and magnesium, which are vital for healthy bones and teeth, make sure that you include low-fat dairy products, wheat germ, almonds, cashews, Brazil nuts, sesame seeds, dark-green leafy vegetables, and tofu in your diet. You will find all these foods in the delicious recipes that follow—*bon appétit*!

immunity *foods*

VITAMIN A AND *zinc are essential nutrients for the immune system. Foods that are rich in zinc include seafood, poultry, eggs, green peas and beans, brown rice, and most legumes. Although vitamin A is found only in animal products, significant amounts of beta carotene, which can be converted into vitamin A by* the body, are found in dark leafy vegetables, carrots, and yellow- or orange-colored fruits such as apricots.

The trace element selenium is also important: good sources are meat, grains, brown rice, seafood, fresh fish, eggs, chicken livers and kidneys, and Brazil nuts. Fresh vegetables and fruits also provide some selenium.

carrot *and* cilantro soup

This tasty carrot soup, served with thick slices of fresh whole-wheat bread, is ideal for a warming lunch or snack. Carrots are high in beta carotene (for vitamin A), which has been linked with lowered rates of cancer and heart disease, and is actually more bioavailable from cooked carrots than from raw.

ingredients

- 1 tbsp olive oil
- 2 onions, chopped
- 1½ pounds (700g) carrots, sliced
- 3½ cups/1½ pints (850ml) vegetable stock (see recipe on page 20)
- sea salt
- freshly ground black pepper
- 2–3tbsp chopped fresh cilantro
- fresh cilantro sprigs, to garnish

serves *four*
preparation time *15 minutes*
cooking time *30 minutes*

method

1 Heat the oil in a large saucepan. Add the onions and cook gently for 5 minutes until softened.
2 Add the carrots, stock, and seasoning. Cover and bring to a boil; then reduce the heat and simmer for 25 minutes, stirring, until the carrots are tender.
3 Remove the pan from the heat and cool slightly; then purée the soup in a food processor.
4 Return the soup to the rinsed-out saucepan. Stir in the chopped cilantro, then reheat gently until piping hot, stirring occasionally.

5 Ladle into warmed soup bowls and garnish with cilantro sprigs.
6 Serve with warm whole-wheat rolls or crispbread.

variations

• *Add the finely grated rind and juice of 1 orange just before serving.*
• *Add 1-2tsp grated fresh, peeled ginger root with the carrots.*

freezing instructions

Let the soup cool completely, then transfer to a rigid, freezerproof container. Cover, seal, and label. Freeze for up to 3 months. Defrost for several hours, or overnight in the refrigerator. Reheat gently in a saucepan until piping hot.

bell pepper, tomato, *and* basil salad

This quick and easy salad makes a colorful and appealing appetizer. Bell peppers and tomatoes contain beta carotene, vitamin C, fiber, and antioxidants, which are beneficial to the immune system.

ingredients

- 2 yellow bell peppers
- 1 red bell pepper
- 1 pound (450g) plum tomatoes
- fresh basil sprigs, to garnish

for the dressing

- 4tbsp olive oil
- 1tbsp balsamic vinegar
- dash of brown sugar
- 2tbsp chopped fresh basil
- sea salt
- freshly ground black pepper

serves *four*
preparation time *15 minutes, plus 1 hour standing time*
cooking time *none*

method

1 Core, seed, and slice the peppers. Slice the tomatoes. Arrange the peppers and tomatoes on a serving platter.
2 To make the dressing, put the oil, vinegar, sugar, basil, and seasoning in a small bowl and whisk together.
3 Drizzle the dressing over the peppers and tomatoes. Cover and leave to stand at room temperature for 1 hour, to let the flavors blend thoroughly.
4 Garnish with fresh basil sprigs.
5 Serve with crusty whole-wheat bread or baked potatoes.

variations

- *Use chopped fresh mixed herbs or chives instead of basil.*

broiled bell peppers *with* goat cheese

A combination of broiled peppers and goat cheese drizzled with a light herbed dressing makes a tasty appetizer. Bell peppers are a good source of beta carotene and vitamin C, both excellent vitamins for boosting the immune system.

■ ingredients

- 2 red bell peppers
- 2 yellow bell peppers
- 8 ounces (225g) goat cheese, diced or sliced
- 16 black olives

for the dressing

- 4tbsp olive oil
- 1–2tbsp chopped fresh mixed herbs
- sea salt
- freshly ground black pepper

serves *four*
preparation time *15 minutes, plus cooling time*
cooking time *10 minutes*

■ method

1 Preheat the broiler to high.

2 Halve, core, and seed the peppers. Place them on a broiler rack in a broiler pan and broil for about 10 minutes, turning occasionally, until the skin is blackened and the flesh softened.

3 Put the peppers in a covered dish and let cool. Remove and discard the skin.

4 Slice the peppers and arrange on four serving plates. Scatter over the cheese.

5 To make the dressing, whisk the oil, herbs, and seasoning in a bowl. Drizzle the oil mixture over the cheese and peppers.

6 Top with black olives.

7 Serve with oven-baked potatoes or whole-wheat bread.

variations

- *Use feta or haloumi cheese instead of goat cheese.*
- *Use chopped fresh basil instead of mixed herbs.*
- *Use half olive and half walnut oil.*

soups   appetizers

warm seafood salad *with* fresh herbs

 This delicious warm salad of mixed dark leaves and seafood is ideal served with crispbread or fresh whole-wheat bread. Shellfish is rich in zinc, which is thought to boost the immune system.

ingredients

- 2 carrots
- 4½ ounces (125g) mixed dark salad leaves such as spinach, lollo rosso, red chard, and mizuna
- 1 tbsp olive oil
- 7-ounce (200g) package frozen small shrimp, defrosted
- 7-ounce (200g) package frozen large shrimp, defrosted

for the dressing

- 4tbsp olive oil
- 1 tbsp unsweetened orange juice
- 2tsp white wine vinegar
- 1 tsp Dijon mustard
- 1–2tbsp chopped fresh mixed herbs
- sea salt
- freshly ground black pepper

serves *four*
preparation time *15 minutes*
cooking time *5 minutes*

method

1 Peel the carrots. Using a potato peeler, shave the carrots thinly. Toss the carrot shavings with the salad leaves and arrange on four serving plates.

2 To make the dressing, put the oil, orange juice, vinegar, mustard, herbs, and seasoning in a bowl and whisk together. Set aside.

3 Heat 1 tbsp oil in a nonstick wok or large skillet. Add the seafood and stir-fry over a high heat for about 5 minutes, until the seafood is cooked.

4 Spoon the cooked seafood over the salad leaves. Give the salad dressing a quick whisk, then drizzle it over the salads.

5 Serve immediately with crispbread or crusty whole-wheat bread.

variations

• *Use zucchini instead of carrots.*

• *Use unsweetened apple juice instead of orange juice.*

• *Use whole-grain mustard instead of Dijon mustard.*

fish *dishes*

peppered salmon *en* papillote

 Salmon remains moist and full of flavor when baked in a paper package. It is rich in vitamin E, which is important for the immune system.

ingredients

- 2–3tbsp mixed peppercorns
- 4 salmon steaks, each weighing about 6 ounces (175g)
- juice of 2 limes

serves *four*
preparation time *10 minutes*
cooking time *20–25 minutes*

method

1 Preheat the oven to 350°F.
2 Crush the peppercorns coarsely using a mortar and pestle, then sprinkle onto a plate. Press each salmon steak into the pepper, covering both sides completely.
3 Cut four pieces of nonstick baking paper, each large enough to hold one salmon steak in a package. Place a salmon steak on each piece of paper and drizzle over some lime juice. Fold the paper over the fish and twist the edges to secure, making four packages.

4 Place the packages on a baking tray and bake for 20–25 minutes, until the fish is cooked and the flesh flakes when tested with a fork.
5 Place each unopened package on a warmed serving plate and serve with cooked fresh vegetables such as new potatoes, broccoli florets, and carrot sticks.

variations

- *Use tuna steaks instead of salmon.*
- *Use lemon juice instead of lime.*

fish *dishes*

lemon chicken kebabs *with* herbed rice

 These flavorsome kebabs are quick to make and delicious to eat. Chicken and brown rice provide zinc, selenium, and B vitamins—good for the immune system and for the healthy growth and repair of cells.

ingredients

- 1 pound (450g) skinless, boneless chicken breasts, cut into 1-inch (2.5cm) cubes
- 2 lemons
- 2tbsp olive oil
- 1 large clove garlic, crushed
- 2tbsp chopped fresh cilantro
- sea salt
- freshly ground black pepper
- 1¼ cups/8 ounces (225g) brown rice
- 2 orange bell peppers, seeded and each cut into 8 pieces
- 16 button mushrooms
- 2–3tbsp chopped fresh mixed herbs

serves *four*
preparation time *20 minutes, plus 1 hour marinating time*
cooking time *35 minutes*

method

1 Put the chicken breasts in a shallow, nonmetallic dish and set aside.

2 Finely grate the rind of 1 lemon and squeeze the juice from both lemons. Place the lemon rind and juice in a small bowl with the oil, garlic, cilantro, and seasoning and whisk together.

3 Pour the marinade over the chicken and toss to coat completely. Cover and refrigerate for 1 hour.

4 Cook the rice in a saucepan of lightly salted, boiling water for about 35 minutes, until tender. Drain well; then rinse with hot water, drain again, and keep hot.

5 Meanwhile, preheat the broiler to medium. Thread the chicken, peppers, and mushrooms onto four long skewers, dividing the ingredients evenly.

6 Place the kebabs on a broiler rack in a broiler pan. Broil for about 10 minutes, turning occasionally, until the chicken is cooked and tender. Brush the kebabs regularly with the marinade to prevent them drying out.

7 Stir the mixed herbs and seasoning into the rice, then spoon the rice into a warmed serving dish. Place the cooked kebabs on top.

8 Serve with a shredded mixed vegetable salad.

variations

- *Use turkey cutlets instead of chicken breasts.*
- *Use sliced zucchini and cherry tomatoes instead of peppers and mushrooms.*
- *Use the rind and juice of a lime instead of lemons.*

deviled chicken livers

The wonderful flavor of chicken livers is highlighted in this tasty recipe. When eaten occasionally, liver is a nutritious food that provides vitamin A, which supports the immune system and is important for skin, eyes, bones, and teeth.

ingredients

- 2tbsp/1 ounce (25g) butter
- 4 shallots, thinly sliced
- 12 ounces chicken livers, sliced
- 8 ounces (225g) mushrooms, sliced
- 2tsp English mustard
- dash of Tabasco sauce
- 2tbsp crème fraîche or light sour cream
- sea salt
- freshly ground black pepper
- 2tbsp chopped fresh parsley, to garnish

serves *four*
preparation time *15 minutes*
cooking time *15 minutes*

method

1 Melt the butter in a large nonstick skillet. Add the shallots and cook gently for 5 minutes, stirring frequently.
2 Add the chicken livers and mushrooms and cook for 5 minutes, stirring occasionally.
3 Stir in the mustard and Tabasco sauce. Cook for another 3–4 minutes, until the livers are cooked, stirring occasionally.
4 Stir in the crème fraîche or light sour cream and reheat gently.
5 Season to taste with salt and pepper and sprinkle with chopped fresh parsley.
6 Serve on a bed of cooked pasta or rice noodles with a mixed dark leaf side salad.

variations

- *Add an extra 1tsp mustard for a slightly hotter sauce.*
- *Use fresh wild mushrooms such as shiitake and oyster mushrooms.*
- *Use 1 leek instead of shallots.*

meat and poultry dishes

fruit *and* nut coleslaw

This combination of lightly dressed vegetables, fruits, and nuts is quick and easy to prepare and makes a great party food. Whole nuts such as Brazils and almonds are good sources of vitamin E and omega-6 essential fatty acids.

ingredients

- 8 ounces (225g) green or white cabbage
- 8 ounces (225g) red cabbage
- 1 large carrot
- 4 celery stalks
- ⅔ cup/4 ounces (115g) raisins
- 1 cup/4 ounces (115g) chopped dried apricots
- 1¼ cups/6 ounces (175g) roughly chopped, mixed Brazil nuts and almonds

for the dressing

- 8tbsp mayonnaise (see recipe on page 21)
- 4tbsp plain yogurt
- 3tbsp chopped fresh mixed parsley and chives
- sea salt
- freshly ground black pepper

serves *six*
preparation time *20 minutes, plus 1–2 hours' chilling time*

method

1 Shred the cabbages, coarsely grate the carrot, and chop the celery. Place in a large bowl. Add the dried fruit and nuts and stir.
2 To make the dressing, mix the mayonnaise, yogurt, herbs, and seasoning together in a small bowl.
3 Spoon the dressing over the cabbage mixture and toss thoroughly. Cover and chill for 1–2 hours before serving.
4 Serve with baked potatoes or slices of crusty whole-wheat bread.

variations

- *Use 6 ounces (175g) sliced mushrooms instead of celery.*
- *Use dried pears, peaches, or mango instead of dried apricots.*
- *Use golden raisins instead of raisins.*

vegetable *dishes*

green vegetable stir-fry *with* pumpkin seeds

The addition of pumpkin seeds, which are rich in zinc, adds flavor and texture to this tasty vegetable stir-fry. Green vegetables provide a wealth of nutrients, including beta carotene (for vitamin A), vitamin C, folic acid, magnesium, and iron.

ingredients

- 8 ounces (225g) small broccoli florets
- 6 ounces (175g) green beans, chopped into 1-inch (2.5cm) lengths
- 2tbsp olive oil
- 1 green bell pepper, seeded and sliced
- 12–16 green onions, chopped
- 1 clove garlic, crushed
- 2 cups/4 ounces (115g) spinach shredded leaves
- 2tbsp dry sherry
- 1tbsp light soy sauce
- 2–3tbsp pumpkin seeds
- sea salt
- freshly ground black pepper

serves *four*
preparation time *15 minutes*
cooking time *10 minutes*

method

1 Blanch the broccoli florets and green beans in a saucepan of boiling water for 2 minutes, then drain thoroughly.

2 Heat the oil in a nonstick wok or large skillet. Add the broccoli, beans, pepper, green onions, and garlic, and stir-fry over a high heat for 3–4 minutes.

3 Add the spinach and stir-fry for another 1–2 minutes.

4 Add the sherry, soy sauce, pumpkin seeds, and seasoning, and stir-fry for 1–2 minutes, until the vegetables are cooked.

5 Serve with baked potatoes or on a bed of brown rice.

variations

• *Use sesame oil instead of olive oil.*

• *Use unsweetened apple juice instead of sherry.*

vegetable *dishes*

root vegetable *and* lentil stew

This thick, wholesome stew of mixed vegetables and lentils is delicious served with brown rice. Lentils are an excellent source of zinc. Root vegetables provide a range of vitamins and minerals, including vitamin C, folic acid, potassium, and magnesium.

■ ingredients

- 1 tbsp olive oil
- 1 onion, sliced
- 1 clove garlic, crushed
- 2 tbsp whole-wheat or potato flour
- 3½ cups/1½ pints (850ml) vegetable stock (see recipe on page 20)
- 1½ cups/8 ounces (225g) diced potatoes
- 1½ cups/8 ounces (225g) carrots, thinly sliced
- 1¼ cups/6 ounces (175g) diced rutabaga
- 1¼ cups/6 ounces (175g) diced parsnips
- 3 celery stalks, chopped
- 1½ cups/8 ounces (225g) whole green or brown lentils
- 1 14-ounce (400g) can chopped tomatoes
- 2 tsp dried mixed herbs
- 1 tsp ground cumin
- sea salt and ground black pepper
- fresh herb sprigs, to garnish

serves *six*
preparation time *15 minutes*
cooking time *55–70 minutes*

■ method

1 Heat the oil in a large saucepan. Add the onion and garlic, and cook for 3 minutes, stirring.
2 Add the flour and cook for 30 seconds, stirring.
3 Remove the pan from the heat, then gradually add the stock, stirring continuously.
4 Add all the remaining ingredients, except the herb garnish, and stir.
5 Bring gently to a boil, stirring continuously. Cover and simmer for 45–60 minutes, until the vegetables and lentils are cooked and tender, stirring occasionally.
6 Adjust the seasoning.
7 Serve on a bed of brown rice or with mashed potatoes, garnished with fresh herb sprigs.

variations

• To cook this dish in the oven, parboil sliced potatoes, then drain thoroughly, and toss in a little olive oil. Bring the stew to a boil, as directed, then transfer to an ovenproof casserole. Arrange the potatoes over the top, covering the vegetable mixture completely. Bake in a preheated oven at 400°F for about 1 hour, until cooked.
• Use sweet potatoes and turnips instead of potatoes and rutabaga. You could also add a few chopped kale leaves for added vitamin C.

freezing instructions

Let cool completely, then transfer to a rigid, freezeproof container. Cover, seal and label. Freeze for up to 3 months. Defrost for and reheat gently in a saucepan until piping hot.

vegetable

fig *and* apple oat crunchies

These oat crunchies make a tasty sweet treat, ideal for a packed lunch or a snack meal. Figs, both fresh and dried, are packed with dietary fiber, iron, magnesium, and calcium.

ingredients

- ½ cup/4 ounces (115g) butter
- ½ cup/4 ounces (115g) light brown sugar
- 2tbsp honey
- 2¼ cups/6 ounces (175g) rolled oats
- 1tsp ground mixed spice
- ½ cup/3 ounces (85g) finely chopped dried figs
- ⅓ cup/1 ounce (25g) finely chopped dried apples

makes *eight to ten*
preparation time *15 minutes*
cooking time *20–30 minutes*

method

1 Preheat the oven to 350°F.
2 Lightly grease a shallow 8-inch square cake pan.
3 Put the butter, sugar, and honey in a saucepan and heat gently until melted. Remove from the heat.
4 Stir in the oats, mixed spice, figs, and apples and mix well. Transfer the mixture to the prepared pan and press it down well.
5 Bake for 20–30 minutes, until golden brown.
6 Mark into fingers or squares while still warm, then let cool completely in the pan. Break into fingers to serve.

variations

- *Use maple syrup instead of honey.*
- *Use muesli, or a mixture of oats and barley or rye flakes.*

freezing instructions

Let cool completely, then wrap in foil or seal in freezer bags and label. Freeze for up to 3 months. Defrost thoroughly for several hours at room temperature before serving.

red fruit molds

These delicious fruit molds are a summertime treat for all the family. Red fruits contain beta carotene (for vitamin A) and vitamin C, antioxidants which may help to boost the immune system.

ingredients

- 1¾ cups/¾ pint (425ml) unsweetened apple juice
- ½ cup/4 ounces (115g) sugar
- juice of 1 lemon
- 1 envelope/¼ ounce (11g) powdered gelatin
- ⅔ cup/¼ pint (150ml) red wine
- 8 ounces (225g) mixed prepared red fruits such as small strawberries and raspberries
- fresh mint sprigs, to decorate

serves *six*
preparation time *15 minutes, plus setting time*
cooking time *10 minutes*

method

1 Put the apple juice and sugar in a saucepan and heat gently, stirring occasionally until the sugar has dissolved. Bring to a boil, then simmer for 5 minutes.
2 Put the lemon juice in a bowl with 2tbsp water and sprinkle over the gelatin. Leave to soak for a couple of minutes; then place the bowl over a pan of simmering water and stir until dissolved.
3 Stir the liquid gelatin and the red wine into the sugar syrup and mix well. Set aside to cool slightly.
4 Arrange the fruits in serving glasses. Pour over a little of the gelatin mixture. Cool slightly, then chill until set.
5 Pour over the remaining liquid jelly. Chill until set.
6 Decorate with fresh mint sprigs and serve with a dollop of yogurt, crème fraîche, or light sour cream.

variations

- *Use white or rosé wine.*
- *Use unsweetened grape juice instead of apple juice.*

desserts *and* bakes

chocolate-dipped fruit *and* nut platter

 This mouthwatering array of chocolate-dipped fruits and whole nuts is hard to resist for a special treat. All fresh fruits contain nutrients that are part of the immune system support group.

ingredients

- 1 pound (450g) fresh firm fruit such as kiwi, pineapple, apricots, peaches, cherries, and strawberries
- 8 squares/8 ounces (225g) dark chocolate
- 8 ounces (225g) whole shelled mixed nuts such as Brazils, almonds, pecans, and cashews

serves *six*
preparation time *30 minutes*

method

1 Line two baking trays with nonstick baking paper and set aside.

2 Peel the kiwi and pineapple. Pit the apricots and peaches. Cut the fruit into slices or wedges, but leave the strawberries whole.

3 Put the chocolate in a small bowl over a pan of hot (but not boiling) water, ensuring that the bottom of the bowl does not touch the water. Stir until the chocolate has melted, then remove the pan from the heat.

4 Make sure the surface of the fruit is dry. Holding one end of a piece of fruit in your fingers, or with a fork, half dip it in the melted chocolate. Lift out and hold over the bowl for a few seconds to drain. Carefully place the dipped fruit onto a prepared baking tray.

5 Repeat with the remaining fruit and the nuts until all the ingredients are used up. Leave to dry completely before removing from the paper.

6 Arrange on a serving platter and serve immediately.

variations

- *Dip ready-to-eat dried fruits such as whole apricots, large raisins, dates, or bananas into melted chocolate.*
- *Dip pieces of candied fruit into melted chocolate.*

an apple *a* day...

ELP KEEP THE *doctor away and stay optimally nourished with this delicious and nutritious immune-boosting menu suggestion* from *the immunity foods section. The vitamins and minerals in these recipes will help your immune system defend against attack by viruses and bacteria.*

carrot *and* cilantro soup

An appetizer rich in beta carotene (for vitamin A), which may help to reduce the risk of cancer and heart disease.

ingredients

- I tbsp olive oil
- 2 onions, chopped
- 1½ pounds (700g) carrots, sliced
- 3½ cups/1½ pints (850ml) vegetable stock (see recipe on page 20)
- sea salt
- freshly ground black pepper
- 2–3tbsp chopped fresh cilantro
- fresh cilantro sprigs, to garnish

serves *four*
preparation time *15 minutes*
cooking time *30 minutes*

method

Heat the oil in a large saucepan. Add the onions and cook gently for 5 minutes until softened.

Add the carrots, stock, and seasoning. Cover and bring to a boil; then reduce the heat and simmer for 25 minutes, stirring, until the carrots are tender.

Remove the pan from the heat and cool slightly; then purée the soup in a food processor.

Return the soup to the rinsed-out saucepan. Stir in the chopped cilantro, then reheat gently until piping hot, stirring occasionally.

Ladle into warmed soup bowls and garnish with cilantro sprigs.

Serve with warm whole-wheat bread or crispbread.

lemon chicken kebabs *with* herbed rice

Chicken and brown rice are a valuable source of zinc, selenium, and B vitamins—immune-boosting essentials and important for the healthy growth and repair of cells.

ingredients

- I pound (450g) skinless, boneless chicken breasts, cut into I-inch (2.5cm) cubes
- 2 lemons
- 2 tbsp olive oil
- I large clove garlic, crushed
- 2 tbsp chopped fresh cilantro
- sea salt
- freshly ground black pepper
- 1¼ cups/8 ounces (225g) brown rice
- 2 orange bell peppers, seeded and each cut into 8 pieces
- 16 button mushrooms
- 2–3 tbsp chopped fresh mixed herbs

serves *four*
preparation time *20 minutes, plus 1 hour marinating time*
cooking time *35 minutes*

method

1 Put the chicken breasts in a shallow, nonmetallic dish and set aside.

2 Finely grate the rind of 1 lemon and squeeze the juice from both lemons. Place the lemon rind and juice in a small bowl with the oil, garlic, cilantro, and seasoning and whisk together.

3 Pour the marinade over the chicken and toss to coat completely. Cover and refrigerate for 1 hour.

4 Cook the rice in a saucepan of lightly salted, boiling water for about 35 minutes, until tender. Drain well; then rinse with hot water, drain again, and keep hot.

5 Meanwhile, preheat the broiler to medium. Thread the chicken, peppers, and mushrooms onto four long skewers, dividing the ingredients evenly.

6 Place the kebabs on a broiler rack in a broiler pan. Broil for about 10 minutes, turning occasionally, until the chicken is cooked and tender. Brush the kebabs regularly with the marinade to prevent them drying out.

7 Stir the mixed herbs and seasoning into the rice, then spoon the rice into a warmed serving dish. Place the cooked kebabs on top.

8 Serve with a shredded mixed vegetable salad.

red fruit molds

All fresh fruits are vital to improve resistance to infection.

ingredients

- 1¾ cups/¾ pint (425ml) unsweetened apple juice
- ½ cup/4 ounces (115g) sugar
- juice of 1 lemon
- 1 envelope/¼ ounce (11g) powdered gelatin
- ⅔ cup/¼ pint (150ml) red wine
- 8 ounces (225g) mixed prepared red fruits such as small strawberries and raspberries
- fresh mint sprigs, to decorate

serves *six*
preparation time *15 minutes, plus setting time*
cooking time *10 minutes*

method

1 Put the apple juice and sugar in a saucepan and heat gently, stirring occasionally until the sugar has dissolved. Bring to a boil, then simmer for 5 minutes.

2 Put the lemon juice in a bowl with 2tbsp water and sprinkle over the gelatin. Leave to soak for a couple of minutes; then place the bowl over a pan of simmering water and stir until dissolved.

3 Stir the liquid gelatin and the red wine into the sugar syrup and mix well. Set aside to cool slightly.

4 Arrange the fruits in serving glasses. Pour over a little of the gelatin mixture. Cool slightly, then chill until set.

5 Pour over the remaining liquid jelly. Chill until set.

6 Decorate with fresh mint sprigs and serve with a dollop of yogurt, crème fraîche, or light sour cream.

heart *and* circulation foods

OMEGA-3 ESSENTIAL FATTY *acids are vital to healthy heart function because they inhibit blood clotting, control cholesterol, and reduce the risk of thrombosis. Oily fish are the main source, but walnuts and seeds also contain significant amounts.*

Vitamin C maintains healthy blood vessels and protects vitamin E (an important antioxidant, which helps protect against heart disease) from free radical damage. Vitamin E-rich foods include whole grains, nuts, and oils. Calcium, magnesium, and selenium are all vital for a healthy heart.

asparagus *and* broccoli scramble

 Green vegetables such as broccoli and asparagus are excellent sources of fiber and vitamin C.

ingredients

- 3 ounces (85g) small broccoli florets
- 3 ounces (85g) asparagus, cut into 1-inch (2.5cm) lengths
- 2tbsp/1 ounce (25g) butter
- 1 leek, washed and thinly sliced
- 8 medium-sized eggs
- 4tbsp milk
- 2tbsp chopped fresh mixed herbs
- sea salt
- freshly ground black pepper
- ¼ cup/1 ounce (25g) finely grated, fresh Parmesan cheese
- 1tbsp toasted sesame seeds
- fresh herb sprigs, to garnish

serves *four*
preparation time *10 minutes*
cooking time *15 minutes*

method

1 Cook the broccoli and asparagus in a saucepan of boiling water for about 4 minutes, until tender. Drain and keep warm.
2 Melt the butter in a pan, and add the leeks. Cook for about 10 minutes, stirring occasionally, until softened.
3 Break the eggs into a bowl and lightly beat them with the milk, chopped herbs, and seasoning. Pour the egg mixture into the pan and cook gently, stirring, until the mixture begins to thicken.
4 Remove the pan from the heat and continue stirring until the mixture becomes creamy.
5 Stir in the broccoli, asparagus, and cheese.

6 Serve hot, sprinkled with sesame seeds. Garnish with the herb sprigs.
7 Serve with slices of whole-wheat bread or toast.

variations

- *Use sunflower or celery seeds instead of sesame seeds.*
- *Use sliced zucchini instead of asparagus.*
- *Use Cheddar cheese instead of Parmesan cheese.*

soups *and* appetizers

brussels sprouts *and* leek soup

 Ideal for chilly winter days, this low-fat, tasty, and filling soup is great for a heart-healthy diet. Brussels sprouts are also a good source of vitamin C.

ingredients

- 1 tbsp olive oil
- 6 shallots, chopped
- 8 ounces (225g) leeks, washed and thinly sliced
- 2½ cups/12 ounces (350g) diced potatoes
- 10 ounces (280g) small Brussels sprouts, quartered
- 3½ cups/1½ pints (850ml) vegetable stock (see recipe on page 20)
- sea salt
- freshly ground black pepper
- 2 tbsp chopped fresh parsley
- flatleaf parsley sprigs, to garnish

serves *four*
preparation time *15 minutes*
cooking time *25–30 minutes*

method

1 Heat the oil in a large saucepan. Cook the shallots for 3 minutes.
2 Add the leeks, potatoes, and Brussels sprouts. Cook for 5 minutes, stirring occasionally.
3 Stir in the stock and seasoning; then cover and bring to a boil. Reduce the heat and simmer for 15–20 minutes, until tender.
4 Cool slightly, then purée in a food processor. Return the soup to the saucepan and reheat.
5 Stir in the chopped parsley and garnish with parsley sprigs.
6 Serve with whole-wheat bread.

variations

• *For a spicy variation, add 2–3tsp curry paste with the stock.*
• *Use sweet potatoes instead of potatoes.*

freezing instructions

Let cool completely, then transfer to a rigid, freezeproof container. Cover, seal, and label. Freeze for up to 3 months. Defrost and reheat gently.

crab-stuffed avocado

Avocados are high in monounsaturated fats that help keep cholesterol counts down. Crab contains selenium, a major antioxidant.

ingredients

- 1¾ cups/8 ounces (225g) flaked crabmeat
- 3 green onions, finely chopped
- 1 tbsp chopped fresh mixed herbs
- 4 tbsp mayonnaise (see recipe on page 21)
- 3 tbsp plain yogurt
- sea salt
- freshly ground black pepper
- 2 ripe avocados
- lemon juice, for brushing
- paprika and lemon wedges, to garnish

serves *four*
preparation time *15 minutes*

method

1 Put the crabmeat, green onions, and herbs in a bowl and mix.
2 In a separate bowl, mix together the mayonnaise and yogurt; then add to the crab mixture and stir. Season to taste with salt and pepper.
3 Halve the avocados lengthways and remove the pits. Place each avocado half on a serving plate and brush the cut surfaces with a little lemon juice to prevent discoloration.
4 Pile the crab mixture into the avocado halves. Garnish with a sprinkling of paprika and lemon wedges, and serve with fingers of lightly buttered, whole-wheat bread or toast.

variations

• *Use canned tuna or salmon or shelled shrirmp instead of crabmeat.*
• *If fresh crabmeat is not available, use two 6-ounce cans crabmeat, drained and flaked.*

thai-spiced tiger shrimp *with* tomato salsa

These Thai-spiced shrimp served with a delicious tomato salsa will be a popular choice for anyone who enjoys seafood. Shrimp are an important source of selenium, which helps to maintain a healthy heart.

▌ ingredients

for the salsa

- 1¾ cups/1 pound (450g) peeled, seeded, and finely chopped tomatoes

- 4 sun-dried tomatoes (not oil-packed), soaked in warm water, drained, and finely chopped

- 2 shallots, finely chopped

- 1 clove garlic, crushed

- 1 tbsp olive oil

- 1–2 tbsp chopped fresh basil

- sea salt

- freshly ground black pepper

for the shrimp kebabs

- 2–3 tsp Thai 7-spice powder

- 2 tbsp olive oil

- 40 raw tiger shrimp, shelled

serves *four*
preparation time *15 minutes, plus 1 hour standing time*
cooking time *4-6 minutes*

▌ method

1 To make the salsa, put the fresh and dried tomatoes, shallots, garlic, olive oil, basil, and seasoning in a bowl and mix well. Cover and leave to stand at room temperature for about 1 hour.

2 Preheat the broiler to high. Put 2 tbsp oil and Thai 7-spice powder in a bowl. Add the shrimp and toss to coat them all over. Thread the shrimp onto four skewers.

3 Place the kebabs on a broiler rack in a broiler pan. Broil for 2–3 minutes on each side, turning occasionally. The shrimp will turn pink once they are cooked.

4 Serve the kebabs hot with the tomato salsa spooned alongside and a crisp green side salad.

variations

- *Use fresh shelled scallops instead of tiger shrimp.*
- *Use 4 green onions instead of the shallots.*
- *Use chopped fresh cilantro or flatleaf parsley instead of basil.*

fish *dishes*

sweet *and* sour turkey meatballs

Turkey meatballs, cooked in a tasty sauce, served with mashed potatoes and fresh vegetables, will be a family favorite. Garlic adds delicious flavor to the meatballs, and is thought to help reduce the risk of heart disease by reducing cholesterol levels and lowering blood pressure.

ingredients

for the meatballs

- 4 cups/1 pound (450g) lean, ground turkey
- 4 shallots, finely chopped
- 1 clove garlic, crushed
- 1¼ cups/4 ounces (115g) finely chopped mushrooms
- 2tsp dried *herbes de provence*
- finely grated rind of 1 lemon
- 1 cup/2 ounces (55g) fresh whole-wheat bread crumbs
- 2tbsp sun-dried tomato paste
- sea salt
- freshly ground black pepper
- a little whole-wheat flour, for dusting
- 1tbsp olive oil

for the sweet and sour sauce

- 1tbsp cornstarch
- 4tbsp red wine
- 1 14-ounce (400g) can chopped tomatoes, puréed
- ⅔ cup/¼ pint (150ml) unsweetened apple juice
- 2tbsp red wine vinegar
- 2tbsp brown sugar
- 1tbsp sun-dried tomato paste
- fresh herb sprigs, to garnish

serves *four to six*
preparation time *25 minutes, plus 20 minutes' chilling time*
cooking time *45 minutes*

method

1 To make the meatballs, put all the meatball ingredients, except the flour and oil, in a bowl and mix thoroughly.

2 Roll the meatball mixture into 28 small balls. Sprinkle the flour onto a plate. Roll each meatball lightly in the flour. Place on a plate, cover, and chill for 20 minutes.

3 Meanwhile, make the sweet and sour sauce. Blend the cornstarch with the red wine; then put in a saucepan with all the remaining sauce ingredients and stir. Bring to a boil, stirring continuously; then reduce the heat and simmer gently while cooking the meatballs.

4 Preheat the oven to 350°F.

5 Heat the oil in a skillet and fry the meatballs over a medium heat for 5–10 minutes, turning them frequently, until lightly browned all over. Transfer the meatballs to a large, shallow, ovenproof dish.

6 Pour the sauce over the meatballs. Cover and bake for about 45 minutes, until the meatballs are cooked.

7 Garnish with fresh herb sprigs and serve hot with mashed potatoes and cooked spring greens and baby carrots.

variations

- *Use ground lean chicken or lamb instead of turkey.*
- *Use 1 small onion instead of the shallots.*
- *Use zucchini instead of mushrooms.*

sweet *and* sour turkey meatballs

Turkey meatballs, cooked in a tasty sauce, served with mashed potatoes and fresh vegetables, will be a family favorite. Garlic adds delicious flavor to the meatballs, and is thought to help reduce the risk of heart disease by reducing cholesterol levels and lowering blood pressure.

ingredients

for the meatballs

- 4 cups/1 pound (450g) lean, ground turkey
- 4 shallots, finely chopped
- 1 clove garlic, crushed
- 1¼ cups/4 ounces (115g) finely chopped mushrooms
- 2tsp dried *herbes de provence*
- finely grated rind of 1 lemon
- 1 cup/2 ounces (55g) fresh whole-wheat bread crumbs
- 2tbsp sun-dried tomato paste
- sea salt
- freshly ground black pepper
- a little whole-wheat flour, for dusting
- 1tbsp olive oil

for the sweet and sour sauce

- 1tbsp cornstarch
- 4tbsp red wine
- 1 14-ounce (400g) can chopped tomatoes, puréed
- ⅔ cup/¼ pint (150ml) unsweetened apple juice
- 2tbsp red wine vinegar
- 2tbsp brown sugar
- 1tbsp sun-dried tomato paste
- fresh herb sprigs, to garnish

serves *four to six*
preparation time *25 minutes, plus 20 minutes' chilling time*
cooking time *45 minutes*

method

1 To make the meatballs, put all the meatball ingredients, except the flour and oil, in a bowl and mix thoroughly.

2 Roll the meatball mixture into 28 small balls. Sprinkle the flour onto a plate. Roll each meatball lightly in the flour. Place on a plate, cover, and chill for 20 minutes.

3 Meanwhile, make the sweet and sour sauce. Blend the cornstarch with the red wine; then put in a saucepan with all the remaining sauce ingredients and stir. Bring to a boil, stirring continuously; then reduce the heat and simmer gently while cooking the meatballs.

4 Preheat the oven to 350°F.

5 Heat the oil in a skillet and fry the meatballs over a medium heat for 5–10 minutes, turning them frequently, until lightly browned all over. Transfer the meatballs to a large, shallow, ovenproof dish.

6 Pour the sauce over the meatballs. Cover and bake for about 45 minutes, until the meatballs are cooked.

7 Garnish with fresh herb sprigs and serve hot with mashed potatoes and cooked spring greens and baby carrots.

variations

- *Use ground lean chicken or lamb instead of turkey.*
- *Use 1 small onion instead of the shallots.*
- *Use zucchini instead of mushrooms.*

chicken *and* mixed pepper stir-fry

 For those in a hurry, this tasty stir-fry is quick to make and is good served with noodles or rice. Sweet bell peppers are super-high in vitamin C.

ingredients

- I tbsp olive oil
- I large clove garlic, finely chopped
- I-inch (2.5cm) piece fresh ginger root, peeled and finely chopped
- 12 ounces (350g) skinless, boneless chicken breast, cut into strips
- I red bell pepper, seeded and sliced
- I yellow bell pepper, seeded and sliced
- I green bell pepper, seeded and sliced
- I zucchini, thinly sliced diagonally
- I leek, washed and thinly sliced
- 4 ounces (115g) sugar-snap peas
- 2–3tsp cajun seasoning or Chinese 5-spice powder
- 2tbsp dry sherry
- I tbsp light soy sauce
- sea salt
- freshly ground black pepper
- toasted sesame seeds, to garnish

serves *four*
preparation time *20 minutes*
cooking time *8–10 minutes*

method

I Heat the oil in a nonstick wok or large skillet. Add the garlic and ginger and stir-fry over a high heat for 30 seconds.

2 Add the chicken and stir-fry for I–2 minutes, until colored all over. Add the peppers, zucchini, leeks, and sugar-snap peas and stir-fry for another 2–3 minutes.

3 Add the cajun seasoning or 5-spice powder, sherry, soy sauce, salt, and pepper, and stir-fry for another 3–4 minutes, until the chicken and vegetables are cooked and tender.

4 Sprinkle with sesame seeds to garnish and serve hot with rice or noodles.

variations

- *Use turkey breast instead of chicken breast.*
- *Use sliced mushrooms instead of sugar-snap peas.*
- *Use unsweetened apple juice instead of sherry.*

pasta primavera

Freshly cooked pasta topped with a tasty and nutritious vegetable sauce makes this recipe a filling lunch or evening meal. Pasta with mixed vegetables is an excellent source of antioxidants and fiber.

ingredients

- 2 carrots, diced
- 2 zucchini, sliced
- 8 ounces (225g) small broccoli florets
- 4 ounces (115g) asparagus, cut into 1-inch (2.5cm) lengths
- 1 cup/6 ounces (175g) frozen peas
- 6–8 green onions, chopped
- 1 clove garlic, crushed
- 1 14-ounce (400g) can chopped tomatoes
- 2/3 cup/1/4 pint (150ml) vegetable stock (see recipe on page 20)
- sea salt
- freshly ground black pepper
- 1 tbsp chopped fresh parsley
- 1 tbsp chopped fresh basil
- 12 ounces (350g) pasta twists (spirals)
- finely grated, fresh Parmesan cheese, to serve

serves *four*
preparation time *15 minutes*
cooking time *25 minutes*

method

1 Put the carrots, zucchini, broccoli, asparagus, peas, green onions, garlic, tomatoes, stock, and seasoning in a saucepan, and bring to a boil, stirring occasionally.
2 Reduce the heat, cover, and simmer for 10 minutes, stirring occasionally. Uncover, increase the heat slightly, and cook for another 5–10 minutes, until the vegetables are cooked and tender, stirring occasionally. Stir the herbs into the vegetable mixture.
3 Meanwhile, cook the pasta in a large saucepan of lightly salted, boiling water for 8–10 minutes, until cooked or *al dente*. Drain the pasta thoroughly.
4 Spoon the pasta onto four warmed serving plates, and spoon the vegetable sauce on top. Serve hot, with Parmesan cheese.
5 Serve with crusty whole-wheat bread or rolls.

variations

- *Use mushrooms instead of asparagus.*
- *Use 1 1/4 cups/6 ounces (175g) diced rutabaga or turnip instead of carrots.*

freezing instructions

The vegetable sauce is suitable for freezing. Let cool completely, then transfer to a rigid, freezeproof container. Cover, seal, and label. Freeze for up to 3 months. Defrost and reheat gently in a saucepan until piping hot. Serve with freshly cooked pasta.

vegetable *dishes*

spicy root vegetables

Root vegetables cooked with spices are a great accompaniment to broiled fish or lean meat. Sweet potatoes are an excellent source of beta carotene, an important antioxidant.

■ ingredients

- 2¼ pounds (1 kg) mixed root vegetables, such as potatoes, sweet potatoes, parsnips, rutabaga, and celeriac, diced
- 3tbsp olive oil
- 1 large clove garlic, crushed
- 1tsp each hot chili powder, ground cumin, and ground coriander
- 2tbsp sunflower or pumpkin seeds (optional)
- sea salt
- freshly ground black pepper
- 2tbsp chopped fresh cilantro

serves *four*
preparation time *15 minutes*
cooking time *15–20 minutes*

■ method

1 Parboil the root vegetables in a large saucepan of boiling water for 5–7 minutes. Drain thoroughly.
2 Heat the oil in a large nonstick skillet. Add the garlic and ground spices, and cook for 30 seconds, stirring.
3 Add the root vegetables and toss in the oil and spice mixture; then cook over a medium heat for 10–15 minutes, stirring frequently, until the vegetables are cooked, tender, and lightly browned.
4 Add the sunflower or pumpkin seeds, if using, and cook for 1–2 minutes. Season to taste and pepper, and stir in the cilantro.
5 Serve hot with broiled fish or lean meat and cooked fresh vegetables such as cabbage and green beans.

variations

• *Use sesame seeds instead of sunflower or pumpkin seeds.*
• *Use chopped fresh flatleaf parsley instead of cilantro.*

onion *and* pepper pizza

This homemade pizza, piled high with a mixed pepper and onion topping, makes an appetizing snack or lunch dish. Onions are a good source of organic sulfur compounds, which have been linked with lowering blood cholesterol and blood pressure.

■ ingredients

for the pizza topping

- 1tbsp olive oil
- 2 medium-sized onions, sliced
- 2 red bell peppers, seeded and sliced
- 6 ounces (175g) cremini mushrooms, sliced
- 1 8-ounce (225g) can chopped tomatoes, drained
- 2tbsp tomato paste
- 2tbsp chopped fresh mixed herbs
- sea salt
- freshly ground black pepper
- 1¼ cups/5 ounces (140g) grated Cheddar cheese

for the pizza base

- 2 cups/8 ounces (225g) plain whole-wheat flour
- dash of salt
- 2tsp baking powder
- ¼ cup/2 ounces (55g) butter
- scant ½ cup/3½ fluid ounces (100ml) milk

serves *four to six*
preparation time *25 minutes*
cooking time *25–30 minutes*

■ method

1 Preheat the oven to 425°F. Line a baking tray with paper.
2 Heat the oil in a saucepan. Add the onions, peppers, and mushrooms; cover and cook gently for 10 minutes.
3 Put the flour, salt, and baking powder in a bowl and rub in the butter until the mixture resembles bread crumbs. Add enough milk to make a soft dough.
4 Roll the dough out on a lightly floured surface to a 10-inch diameter circle. Place the dough on the baking tray.
5 Mix the tomatoes and tomato purée together and spread over the base. Sprinkle over the herbs and seasoning.
6 Add the onion mixture and sprinkle on the cheese.
7 Bake for 25–30 minutes.
8 Serve hot or cold, in slices.

variations

• *Use 8 shallots instead of onions.*
• *Use sliced zucchini instead of mushrooms.*

baked bananas *with* cinnamon

This delicious dessert of baked bananas is especially good served with a dollop of crème fraîche, light sour cream, or yogurt. Bananas are rich in potassium, which is important for maintaining proper blood pressure.

ingredients

- 4tbsp unsweetened orange juice
- 4tbsp honey
- 2tbsp rum
- 4 firm, ripe bananas
- 2 cinnamon sticks, broken in half

serves *four*
preparation time *10 minutes*
cooking time *30 minutes*

method

1 Preheat the oven to 350°F.
2 Put the orange juice, honey, and rum in a small bowl and mix well.
3 Peel the bananas and slice each one in half lengthways. Put the banana halves in a shallow, ovenproof dish. Add the broken cinnamon sticks.
4 Pour over the orange juice mixture and turn the bananas over in the mixture.
5 Cover the dish with foil and bake for about 30 minutes, until the bananas are softened.
6 Remove and discard the cinnamon sticks. Serve the bananas on warmed serving plates with the sauce spooned over.
7 Add a dollop of crème fraîche, light sour cream, or yogurt, or a scoop of homemade yogurt ice.

variations

• *For spicy baked bananas, omit the cinnamon and add 2tsp ground mixed spice to the orange juice mixture before baking.*
• *Use fresh peaches or nectarines instead of bananas.*
• *Use maple syrup instead of honey.*
• *Use brandy instead of rum.*
• *For extra selenium and EFAs, sprinkle raw wheatgerm and linseeds over the top.*

desserts *and* bakes

fruit kebabs *with* lemon sauce

Fresh fruit kebabs served with a tangy lemon sauce make an ideal light dessert. Kiwi fruit and strawberries are good sources vitamin C, which promotes iron absorption and maintains healthy blood vessels.

■ ingredients

- 1 pound (450g) small strawberries
- 6 kiwi fruit, peeled and each cut into 8 pieces

for the lemon sauce

- 2tsp arrowroot
- finely grated rind and juice of 2 lemons
- 4tbsp honey
- fresh mint sprigs, to decorate

serves *four*
preparation time *10 minutes*
cooking time *10 minutes*

■ method

1 Thread the strawberries and kiwi fruit onto four long or eight short skewers, dividing the fruit evenly between the skewers. Place on four serving plates and set aside.

2 Blend the arrowroot with 3tbsp water and put into a saucepan with the lemon rind, juice, and honey.

3 Bring slowly to a boil, stirring, until the mixture thickens.

4 Serve the lemon sauce drizzled over or alongside the fruit kebabs. Decorate with fresh mint sprigs.

5 Serve with homemade fruit yogurt ice for a special treat.

variations
• *The lemon sauce can be served hot or cold.*
• *Replace the strawberries and kiwi fruit with other fresh fruit such as papaya, grapes, mango, pineapple, nectarines, or eating apples.*
• *Use lime juice instead of lemon.*

desserts *and* bakes

the hungry heart

CONTROL CHOLESTEROL LEVELS, *and get your heart and circulation going with this stimulating selection of recipes from the heart and circulation section, rich in the nutrients vitamin E, omega-3 and -6 essential fatty acids, vitamin C, and potassium—all vital for healthy heart and circulation.*

crab-stuffed avocado

Avocado is rich in vitamin E and crab contains selenium—both essential antioxidants, which could help to protect against heart disease.

ingredients

- 1¾ cups/8 ounces (225g) flaked crabmeat
- 3 green onions, finely chopped
- 1 tbsp chopped fresh mixed herbs
- 4 tbsp mayonnaise (see recipe on page 21)
- 3 tbsp plain yogurt
- sea salt
- freshly ground black pepper
- 2 ripe avocados
- lemon juice, for brushing
- paprika and lemon wedges, to garnish

serves *four*
preparation time *15 minutes*

method

1 Put the crabmeat, green onions, and herbs in a bowl and mix.
2 In a separate bowl, mix together the mayonnaise and yogurt; then add to the crab mixture and stir. Season to taste with salt and pepper.
3 Halve the avocados lengthways and remove the pits. Place each avocado half on a serving plate and brush the cut surfaces with a little lemon juice to prevent discoloration.
4 Pile the crab mixture into the avocado halves. Garnish with a sprinkling of paprika and lemon wedges, and serve with fingers of lightly buttered, whole-wheat bread or toast.

chicken *and* mixed pepper stir-fry

Olive oil is a valuable source of mono-unsaturated fat and the peppers are rich in vitamin C, which promotes iron absorption and maintains healthy blood vessels.

ingredients

- 1 tbsp olive oil
- 1 large clove garlic, finely chopped
- 1-inch (2.5cm) piece fresh ginger root, peeled and finely chopped
- 12 ounces (350g) skinless, boneless chicken breast, cut into strips
- 1 red bell pepper, seeded and sliced
- 1 yellow bell pepper, seeded and sliced
- 1 green bell pepper, seeded and sliced

- 1 zucchini, thinly sliced diagonally
- 1 leek, washed and thinly sliced
- 4 ounces (115g) sugar-snap peas
- 2–3tsp cajun seasoning or Chinese 5-spice powder
- 2tbsp dry sherry
- 1tbsp light soy sauce
- sea salt
- freshly ground black pepper
- toasted sesame seeds, to garnish

serves *four*
preparation time *20 minutes*
cooking time *8–10 minutes*

method

1 Heat the oil in a nonstick wok or large skillet. Add the garlic and ginger and stir-fry over a high heat for 30 seconds.
2 Add the chicken and stir-fry for 1–2 minutes, until colored all over. Add the peppers, zucchini, leeks, and sugar-snap peas and stir-fry for another 2–3 minutes.
3 Add the cajun seasoning or 5-spice powder, sherry, soy sauce, salt, and pepper, and stir-fry for another 3–4 minutes, until the chicken and vegetables are cooked and tender.
4 Sprinkle with sesame seeds to garnish and serve hot with rice or noodles.

baked bananas *with* cinnamon

Bananas make this dessert rich in potassium, a mineral instrumental in maintaining proper muscle function and blood pressure.

ingredients

- 4tbsp unsweetened orange juice
- 4tbsp honey
- 2tbsp rum
- 4 firm, ripe bananas
- 2 cinnamon sticks, broken in half

serves *four*
preparation time *10 minutes*
cooking time *30 minutes*

method

1 Preheat the oven to 350°F.
2 Put the orange juice, honey, and rum in a small bowl and mix well.
3 Peel the bananas and slice each one in half lengthways. Put the banana halves in a shallow, ovenproof dish. Add the broken cinnamon sticks.
4 Pour over the orange juice mixture and turn the bananas over in the mixture.
5 Cover the dish with foil and bake for about 30 minutes, until the bananas are softened.
6 Remove and discard the cinnamon sticks. Serve the bananas on warmed serving plates with the sauce spooned over.
7 Add a dollop of crème fraîche, light sour cream, or yogurt, or a scoop of homemade yogurt ice.

foods for teeth *and* bones

CALCIUM IS A CRUCIAL *component of bones and teeth, the best food sources are dairy products, canned fish (with bones), and some dark-green leafy vegetables. Vitamin D, found in oily fish, promotes absorption of calcium into the bloodstream. Magnesium is* also vital for healthy bones and teeth. Good sources include bananas, brown rice, fish, green vegetables, nuts, pasta, and legumes. Beta carotene, which the body can convert to vitamin A, is found in dark leafy vegetables, carrots, and yellow or orange fruits.

roasted baby vegetables

 This nutritious appetizer is easy to make. A grated cheese topping gives the vegetables a calcium boost for healthy bones and teeth.

ingredients

- 10 ounces (280g) baby zucchini
- 10 ounces (280g) baby eggplants
- 8 ounces (225g) baby corn
- 8 ounces (225g) baby onions or shallots, halved
- 8 ounces (225g) button mushrooms
- 2 cloves garlic, thinly sliced
- 2tbsp olive oil
- 9 ounces (250g) cherry tomatoes
- 1tbsp each chopped fresh thyme and parsley
- sea salt and pepper
- 3–4tbsp French dressing (see recipe on page 21)
- grated cheddar cheese, to garnish

serves *four*
preparation time *10 minutes*
cooking time *30 minutes*

method

1 Preheat the oven to 425°F.
2 Put the zucchini, eggplants, corn, onions or shallots, mushrooms, and garlic in a large roasting pan. Drizzle over the oil and toss well.
3 Bake for 20 minutes, stirring once or twice.
4 Stir in the tomatoes, herbs and seasoning. Bake for another 5–10 minutes, until the vegetables are cooked and are just beginning to brown at the edges.
5 Sprinkle the cooked vegetables with the French dressing and top with grated Cheddar cheese.

variations

• *Top the cooked vegetables with grated Cheddar or mozzarella cheese and place under a hot broiler until melted.*
• *Use chopped fresh basil or marjoram instead of thyme.*

melon *and* kiwi cocktail

This light and tasty appetizer can be served on its own or with crispbread. Kiwi fruit are a good source of vitamin C and potassium, vital for bones.

ingredients

- 1 medium-size orange- or yellow-fleshed melon
- 4 kiwi fruit
- ²/₃ cup/¼ pint (150ml) unsweetened apple or grape juice
- 1–2tbsp fruit liqueur or brandy
- fresh mint sprigs, to garnish

serves *four*
preparation time *10 minutes, plus 1 hour standing time*

method

1 Halve the melon; remove and discard the seeds. Peel the melon and chop the flesh into bite-size pieces. Put into a bowl.
2 Peel the kiwi fruit and dice the flesh. Add to the chopped melon and stir.
3 Mix together the apple or grape juice and liqueur or brandy. Pour over the fruit and stir to mix. Cover and set aside for about 1 hour to allow the flavors to blend.
4 Spoon the fruit and juices into four serving dishes and garnish with fresh mint sprigs.

variations

- Use a melon baller to make balls instead of cubes.
- Use a pineapple instead of a melon.
- Use 8 ounces (225g) strawberries, halved, instead of the kiwi fruit.

hot spinach soufflé

This tasty savory soufflé will be enjoyed by all the family. Spinach is a good source of magnesium, beta carotene, and folic acid.

ingredients

- 1tbsp finely grated fresh Parmesan cheese
- 1 pound (450g) spinach leaves, washed and roughly chopped
- 2tbsp/1 ounce (25g) butter
- ¼ cup/1 ounce (25g) whole-wheat flour
- 1 cup/9 fluid ounces (250ml) milk
- 4 medium-sized eggs, separated, plus 1 extra egg white
- 1 cup/4 ounces (115g) grated Cheddar cheese
- dash of cayenne pepper
- sea salt
- freshly ground black pepper

serves *four to six*
preparation time *20 minutes*
cooking time *30–45 minutes*

method

1 Preheat the oven to 375°F.
2 Lightly grease a 3½-pint (1.7 liter) soufflé dish. Sprinkle the dish with Parmesan cheese and set aside.
3 Cook the spinach in a little boiling water until just cooked. Drain thoroughly, then chop finely.
4 Put the butter, flour, and milk in a saucepan and heat gently, whisking until the sauce comes to the boil and thickens. Simmer for 2 minutes, stirring.
5 Stir in the spinach.
6 Gradually beat in the egg yolks and ¾ cup cheese. Add the cayenne pepper and seasoning.
7 Whisk the egg whites until stiff, then fold into the spinach mixture.
8 Spoon into the soufflé dish and sprinkle with the remaining cheese. Place on a baking tray and bake for 30–45 minutes, until well-risen, golden brown, and just set.
9 Serve with a mixed leaf salad and whole-wheat bread.

grilled mackerel *with* rosemary

 Lemon and rosemary add flavor to char-grilled mackerel in this delicious recipe. Vitamin D, which occurs naturally in oily fish, promotes the absorption of calcium from the gut to the bloodstream.

■ ingredients

- 4 fresh mackerel, each weighing about 10–12 ounces (280–350g), cleaned and with bones and heads removed
- juice of 2 lemons
- 2tbsp olive oil
- 2tbsp chopped fresh rosemary
- sea salt
- freshly ground black pepper
- fresh rosemary sprigs, to garnish

serves *four*
preparation time *5 minutes, plus 1–2 hours' marinating time*
cooking time *10–12 minutes*

■ method

1 Make two or three diagonal cuts on both sides of each fish. Place in a shallow, nonmetallic dish.
2 Put the lemon juice, oil, rosemary, and seasoning in a small bowl and whisk. Pour the mixture over the fish and turn to coat completely. Cover and refrigerate for 1–2 hours.
3 Preheat the barbecue coals or broiler to medium. Place the mackerel on a broiler rack and cook for 10–12 minutes, until the flesh flakes when tested with a fork. Turn during cooking and brush with the marinade to prevent drying out.
4 Garnish with rosemary sprigs and serve with baked potatoes and homemade coleslaw.

variations

· *Use lime or orange juice instead of lemon.*
· *Use fresh thyme instead of rosemary.*

salmon *and* asparagus risotto

Salmon and asparagus add extra flavor and nutrients to this tasty risotto. Salmon and brown rice both provide magnesium, a crucial mineral for maintaining healthy bones and teeth.

■ ingredients

- 1tbsp olive oil
- 1 onion, chopped
- 2 cloves garlic, finely chopped
- 8 ounces (225g) mushrooms, sliced
- 1¼ cups/8 ounces (225g) brown rice
- 1¼ cups/½ pint (300ml) dry white wine
- 1¾ cups/¾ pint (425ml) boiling vegetable or fish stock (see recipe on page 20)
- 10 ounces (280g) fresh asparagus, chopped into 1-inch (2.5cm) lengths
- 1 14-ounce (400g) can salmon in water, drained and flaked
- 2tbsp chopped fresh tarragon
- sea salt
- freshly ground black pepper

serves *four*
preparation time *15 minutes*
cooking time *40 minutes*

■ method

1 Heat the oil in a saucepan. Add the onion and garlic. Cook for 5 minutes, stirring occasionally.
2 Add the mushrooms and rice. Cook for 1 minute, stirring.
3 Add the wine and a little stock. Bring to a boil, reduce the heat, and simmer, uncovered, until almost all the liquid has been absorbed.
4 Continue adding the hot stock until the rice is cooked and creamy.
5 Meanwhile, steam the asparagus over a saucepan of boiling water for 8–10 minutes, until tender. Drain thoroughly and keep warm.
6 Stir the asparagus, salmon, and tarragon into the risotto. Season to taste, and cook gently until the salmon is hot.
7 Serve with a mixed tomato and bell pepper salad.

variations

· *Use canned tuna instead of salmon.*
· *Use cilantro instead of tarragon.*
· *Use zucchini instead of mushrooms.*

fish *dishes*

lamb *and* apricot pilaf

 This fruity lamb pilaf is sure to be a favorite choice for all the family. Lamb, rice, and cashews provide magnesium, and dried fruits such as apricots provide boron, essential elements for bones and teeth.

ingredients

- 1tbsp olive oil
- 12 ounces (350g) lean lamb, cut into 1-inch (2.5cm) cubes
- 1 onion, chopped
- 1 red bell pepper, seeded and diced
- 1 clove garlic, crushed
- 1-inch (2.5cm) piece ginger root, peeled and finely chopped
- 2tsp ground cumin
- 1tsp ground coriander
- 1¼ cups/8 ounces (225g) long-grain brown rice
- 2 cups/16 fluid ounces (450ml) vegetable stock (see page 20)
- ⅔ cup/¼ pint (150ml) red wine
- sea salt
- freshly ground black pepper
- 1¼ cups/4 ounces (115g) chopped dried apricots
- ½–¾ cup/2–3 ounces (55–85g) unsalted cashews
- fresh cilantro sprigs, to garnish

serves *four*
preparation time *15 minutes*
cooking time *40–45 minutes*

method

1 Heat the oil in a large saucepan. Add the lamb and cook until browned all over. Remove the lamb from the pan using a slotted spoon, set aside, and keep warm.
2 Add the onion, pepper, garlic, and ginger to the pan. Cook for 3 minutes, stirring occasionally.
3 Add the ground spices. Cook for 1 minute, stirring.
4 Return the lamb to the pan; add the rice, stock, wine, and seasoning, and stir. Cover and bring to a boil; then reduce the heat and simmer for 15 minutes, stirring occasionally.
5 Stir in the apricots. Return to a boil, cover, and simmer for another 15–20 minutes, until the lamb is cooked and almost all the liquid has been absorbed.
6 Fold in the cashews, then spoon into a warmed serving dish. Garnish with cilantro sprigs.
7 Serve with cooked fresh vegetables such as spinach and green beans.

variations

- *Use large raisins instead of apricots.*
- *Use flaked or whole almonds instead of cashews.*

freezing instructions

Let cool completely. then transfer to a rigid, freezeproof container. Cover, seal, and label. Freeze for up to 3 months. Defrost completely, then reheat gently in a saucepan until piping hot, adding a little extra stock, if necessary.

meat *and* poultry *dishes*

pan-fried chicken livers
with mushrooms *and* sage

Succulent chicken livers are cooked with mushrooms and fresh sage to create this tasty dish. Liver contains many nutrients, including vitamin A, which is important for healthy bones and teeth.

ingredients

- 1 tbsp/½ ounce (15g) butter
- 1 tbsp olive oil
- 1 onion, sliced
- 1 pound (450g) chicken livers, cut into thin strips
- 8 ounces (225g) small button mushrooms
- 6 tbsp port or red wine
- 1 tbsp chopped fresh sage
- sea salt
- freshly ground black pepper
- fresh sage leaves, to garnish

serves *four to six*
preparation time
10–15 minutes
cooking time *8–10 minutes*

method

1 Heat the butter and oil in a large nonstick skillet until the butter is melted. Add the onion and cook gently for about 10 minutes, stirring occasionally, until the onion is softened.
2 Add the chicken livers, mushrooms, and port or wine. Cook over a medium to low heat for about 10 minutes, until the liver is just cooked, stirring occasionally.
3 Stir in the chopped sage and season to taste.
4 Garnish with fresh sage leaves.
5 Serve with boiled brown rice with cooked fresh vegetables such as peas and carrots.

variations
• *Use sherry or brandy instead of port or red wine.*
• *Use fresh thyme instead of sage.*

country chicken
and barley casserole

This hearty and wholesome casserole makes a tasty and filling dish for winter days. Whole grains such as barley contain magnesium, which helps to strengthen bones and teeth.

ingredients

- 1 tbsp olive oil
- 4 skinless chicken breasts
- 12 ounces (350g) pearl onions, peeled
- 2 leeks, washed and sliced
- 8 ounces (225g) baby carrots
- 8 ounces (225g) button mushrooms
- 2 cups/8 ounces (225g) diced celeriac
- ¼ cup/2 ounces (55g) pearl barley
- 1 14-ounce (400g) can chopped tomatoes
- 2 tbsp tomato paste
- 1¾ cups/¾ pint (425ml) chicken stock (see recipe on page 20)
- 1¼ cups/½ pint (300ml) dry white wine
- 1 bouquet garni
- sea salt
- freshly ground black pepper
- fresh herb sprigs, to garnish

serves *four*
preparation time *15 minutes*
cooking time *1½–2 hours*

method

1 Preheat the oven to 350°F.
2 Heat the oil in a large flameproof and ovenproof casserole. Add the chicken and cook until browned.
3 Stir in all the remaining ingredients. Bring to a boil, cover, and bake for 1½ hours. Remove the bouquet garni.
4 Garnish with fresh herb sprigs.
5 Serve hot with potatoes and broccoli or cauliflower florets.

variations
• *Use turkey instead of chicken.*
• *Use rutabaga instead of celeriac.*
• *Use green split peas instead of pearl barley.*

freezing instructions
Let cool completely, then transfer to a rigid, freezeproof container. Cover, seal, and label. Freeze for up to 3 months. Defrost thoroughly and reheat gently in a moderate oven until piping hot.

tofu *and* vegetable kebabs

A tasty combination of marinated tofu and vegetables ensure these vegetarian kebabs are a popular choice. For a rich source of calcium, choose tofu that is made with calcium chloride.

ingredients

- 3tbsp olive oil
- finely grated rind and juice of 1 lemon
- 1 clove garlic, crushed
- 1tsp each ground cumin and hot chili powder
- 1tbsp chopped fresh mixed herbs
- sea salt
- freshly ground black pepper
- 10 ounces (280g) tofu, cut into small cubes
- 4 shallots, halved
- 1 red bell pepper, seeded and cut into 8 chunks
- 1 zucchini, cut into 16 thin slices
- 16 button mushrooms
- 16 cherry tomatoes

serves *four*
(two kebabs per serving)
preparation time *10 minutes, plus 30 minutes' marinating time*
cooking time *8 minutes*

method

1 Put the olive oil, lemon rind and juice, garlic, spices, herbs, and seasoning in a bowl and whisk.
2 Place the tofu in a shallow, nonmetallic dish, pour over the oil mixture, and toss. Cover and set aside for 30 minutes.
3 Preheat the broiler to high. Thread the tofu and vegetables evenly onto four long or eight short skewers.
4 Place the kebabs on a rack in a broiler pan and broil for 3–4 minutes on each side, until lightly browned, turning frequently. Brush frequently with the marinade mixture.
5 Serve the hot kebabs on a bed of brown rice and with a chopped, mixed side salad.

variations

• *To make a tofu and vegetable stir-fry, marinate the tofu as directed. Heat a little olive oil in a nonstick wok or skillet. Add the tofu and vegetables, and stir-fry for 6–8 minutes. Add the marinade, and stir-fry for 2 minutes; then serve hot.*

spiced vegetable couscous

A spicy vegetable sauce served on a bed of hot couscous makes an appetizing meal. Leafy green vegetables such as broccoli contain calcium and magnesium, both good for bones.

ingredients

- 2tbsp olive oil
- 1 large onion, sliced
- 2 cloves garlic, finely chopped
- 2 zucchini, sliced
- 6 ounces (175g) broccoli florets
- 8 ounces (225g) mushrooms, sliced
- 2 carrots, thinly sliced
- 1 red bell pepper, seeded and sliced
- 1tbsp ground mixed spices such as coriander, cumin, chili, and allspice
- 2½ cups/1 pint (600ml) vegetable stock (see recipe on page 20)
- sea salt
- freshly ground black pepper
- 1¼ cups/8 ounces (225g) frozen peas
- 2–3tbsp cornstarch
- 2 cups/12 ounces (350g) quick-cook couscous
- fresh herb sprigs, to garnish

serves *four to six*
preparation time *15 minutes*
cooking time *25–30 minutes*

method

1 Heat 1tbsp oil in a saucepan. Add all the fresh vegetables and cook gently for 5 minutes.
2 Add the spices and cook for 1 minute, stirring.
3 Add the stock, seasoning, and peas, and stir.
4 Blend the cornstarch with 4–5tbsp water and stir into the vegetable mixture. Bring to a boil, stirring continuously, until the mixture thickens slightly.
5 Reduce the heat, cover, and simmer for 15–20 minutes, until the vegetables are tender.
6 Soak and cook the couscous according to the directions.
7 Stir the remaining oil into the couscous, then spoon it onto warmed serving plates. Spoon the spiced vegetable mixture on top. Garnish with fresh herb sprigs.

variations

• *Choose your own mixture of fresh and frozen vegetables.*
• *Serve the sauce with brown rice or pasta instead of couscous.*
• *Use a lime instead of a lemon.*

vegetable *dishes*

fragrant fruit salad

 This delicious fruit salad is easy to make. Fresh fruits contain vitamin C, fiber, and other antioxidants important for health.

■ ingredients

- 1 small pineapple
- 1 ripe mango
- 1 carambola (star fruit)
- 3 kiwi fruit
- ¾ cup/7 fluid ounces (200ml) unsweetened apple juice
- ¾ cup/7 fluid ounces (200ml) unsweetened orange juice
- 2tbsp sherry
- 2tbsp honey (optional)
- fresh mint sprigs, to decorate

serves *four to six*
preparation time *15 minutes, plus 1 hour standing time*

■ method

1 Peel, core, and chop the pineapple. Peel, pit, and chop the mango. Place in a bowl.

2 Slice the carambola and peel and slice the kiwi fruit. Add to the bowl and stir.

3 Mix together the fruit juices, sherry, and honey, if using. Pour over the fruit in the bowl and stir gently.

4 Cover and leave to stand at room temperature for 1 hour before serving to let the flavors blend.

5 Spoon into bowls to serve and decorate with fresh mint sprigs.

6 Serve with homemade yogurt ice or yogurt.

variations

• *Use other fresh fruit mixtures such as apples, pears, cherries, peaches, and apricots.*

• *Use unsweetened grape or pineapple juice instead of apple or orange juice.*

• *For extra calcium, top with a teaspoon of sesame seeds.*

desserts *and* bakes

fruity breakfast muffins

You can't beat the aroma and flavor of these raspberry muffins, ideal for a breakfast-time treat. Raspberries are a good source of vitamin C, vital for healthy gums and teeth.

ingredients

- 1¾ cups/7 ounces (200g) whole-wheat flour
- 1tbsp baking powder
- pinch of salt
- 1 cup/4 ounces (115g) small fresh raspberries
- ¼ cup/2 ounces (55g) melted butter
- ¼ cup/2 ounces (55g) light brown sugar
- 1 medium-sized egg, beaten
- ¾ cup/7 fluid ounces (200ml) milk

makes *nine muffins*
preparation time *20 minutes*
cooking time *15–20 minutes*

method

1 Preheat the oven to 400°F. Line nine muffin pans with paper cases.
2 Put the flour, baking powder, and salt into a large bowl. Stir in the raspberries.
3 Mix the melted butter, sugar, egg, and milk in a separate bowl; then pour over the flour mixture.
4 Gently fold the ingredients together, and spoon the mixture into the prepared muffin cases, filling each case two-thirds full.
5 Bake for 15–20 minutes until golden brown.
6 Transfer to a wire rack to cool slightly. Serve on their own, or split and spread with a little butter, preserve, honey, or fruit curd.

variations

• *Use other fresh or dried fruit instead of raspberries.*
• *Add the finely grated rind of 1 lemon or orange, or 1–2tsp ground mixed spice, cinnamon, or ginger to the muffin mixture before baking.*

summer strawberry yogurt ice

Yogurt ice is a delicious and nutritious dessert, ideal for summertime eating alfresco. Yogurt is a valuable source of calcium, a fundamental mineral for healthy bones and teeth.

ingredients

- 1 pound strawberries
- ¼ cup/2 ounces (55g) brown sugar
- 1¼ cups/½ pint (300ml) plain yogurt
- 1¼ cups/½ pint (300ml) strawberry yogurt
- fresh mint sprigs, to decorate

serves *six*
preparation time *10 minutes, plus freezing time*

method

1 Put the strawberries in a food processor and blend until smooth. Add the sugar and yogurts. Blend until well mixed.
2 Pour the mixture into a chilled, shallow, plastic container. Cover and freeze for 1½–2 hours, or until the mixture has a mushy consistency. Spoon into a bowl and mash with a fork to break down the ice crystals. Return the mixture to the container, cover, and freeze until firm.
3 Transfer the yogurt ice to the refrigerator 30 minutes to let it soften a little. Scoop the yogurt ice into serving dishes and decorate with the mint sprigs.
4 Serve with fresh fruit such as raspberries or sliced peaches.

variations

• *Replace the strawberries with blackberries and the strawberry yogurt with raspberry yogurt.*
• *Use honey instead of sugar.*

freezing instructions

The yogurt ice will keep for up to 3 months in the freezer.

desserts *and* bakes

bred *in the* bone

TO ENSURE YOU *don't go weak in the knees, there is a scrumptious selection of recipes to nourish and strengthen your bones and* teeth—*this mouthwatering menu contains all those essential vitamins and minerals to help protect the most delicate of frames.*

hot spinach soufflé

Excellent for fighting the damaging effects of free radicals, spinach is a good source of magnesium, beta carotene, and vitamin C—essential nutrients for building strong bones and teeth.

ingredients

- I tbsp finely grated fresh Parmesan cheese
- I pound (450g) spinach leaves, washed and roughly chopped
- 2 tbsp/I ounce (25g) butter
- ¼ cup/I ounce (25g) whole-wheatflour
- I cup/9 fluid ounces (250ml) milk
- 4 medium-sized eggs, separated, plus I extra egg white
- I cup/4 ounces (115g) grated Cheddar cheese
- dash of cayenne pepper
- sea salt
- freshly ground black pepper

serves *four to six*
preparation time *20 minutes*
cooking time *30–45 minutes*

method

1 Preheat the oven to 375°F.
2 Lightly grease a 3½-pint (1.7 liter) soufflé dish. Sprinkle the dish with Parmesan cheese and set aside.
3 Cook the spinach in a little boiling water until just cooked. Drain thoroughly then chop finely.
4 Put the butter, flour, and milk in a saucepan and heat gently, whisking until the sauce comes to the boil and thickens. Simmer for 2 minutes, stirring.
5 Stir in the spinach.
6 Gradually beat in the egg yolks and ¾ cup cheese. Add the cayenne pepper and seasoning.
7 Whisk the egg whites until stiff, then fold into the spinach mixture.
8 Spoon into the soufflé dish and sprinkle with the remaining cheese. Place on a baking tray and bake for 30–45 minutes, until well-risen, golden brown, and just set.
9 Serve with a mixed leaf salad and whole-wheat bread.

salmon *and* asparagus risotto

Both salmon and brown rice are good sources of the magnesium that is needed for healthy bones and teeth.

■ ingredients

- 1tbsp olive oil
- 1 onion, chopped
- 2 cloves garlic, finely chopped
- 8 ounces (225g) mushrooms, sliced
- 1¼ cups/8 ounces (225g) brown rice
- 1¼ cups/½ pint (300ml) dry white wine
- 1¾ cups/¾ pint (425ml) boiling vegetable or fish stock (see recipe on page 20)
- 10 ounces (280g) fresh asparagus, chopped into 1-inch (2.5cm) lengths
- 1 14-ounce (400g) can salmon in water, drained and flaked
- 2tbsp chopped fresh tarragon
- sea salt and ground black pepper

serves *four*
preparation time *15 minutes*
cooking time *40 minutes*

■ method

1 Heat the oil in a saucepan. Add the onion and garlic. Cook for 5 minutes, stirring occasionally.
2 Add the mushrooms and rice. Cook for 1 minute, stirring.
3 Add the wine and a little stock. Bring to a boil, reduce the heat, and simmer, uncovered, until almost all the liquid has been absorbed.
4 Continue adding the hot stock until the rice is cooked and creamy.
5 Meanwhile, steam the asparagus over a saucepan of boiling water for 8–10 minutes, until tender. Drain thoroughly and keep warm.
6 Stir the asparagus, salmon, and tarragon into the risotto. Season to taste, and cook gently until the salmon is hot.
7 Serve with a mixed tomato and bell pepper salad.

fragrant fruit salad

A juicy way to round off this bone-strengthening menu—these fresh fruits provide plenty of vitamin C, good for teeth, bones, and gums.

■ingredients

- 1 small pineapple
- 1 ripe mango
- 1 carambola (star fruit)
- 3 kiwi fruit
- ¾ cup/7 fluid ounces (200ml) unsweetened apple juice
- ¾ cup/7 fluid ounces (200ml) unsweetened orange juice
- 2tbsp sherry
- 2tbsp honey (optional)
- fresh mint sprigs, to decorate

serves *four to six*
preparation time *15 minutes,*
plus 1 hour standing time

■ method

1 Peel, core, and chop the pineapple. Peel, pit, and chop the mango. Place in a bowl.
2 Slice the carambola and peel and slice the kiwi fruit. Add to the bowl and stir.
3 Mix together the fruit juices, sherry, and honey, if using. Pour over the fruit in the bowl and stir gently.
4 Cover and leave to stand at room temperature for 1 hour before serving to let the flavors blend.
5 Spoon into bowls to serve and decorate with fresh mint sprigs.
6 Serve with homemade yogurt ice or yogurt.

flexibility *foods*

FOR FLEXIBLE JOINTS, *antioxidants such as vitamin C and beta carotene are important— good sources of these include green, yellow, orange, and red fruits and vegetables. Selenium may also be an important nutrient for healthy joints. The* best sources of this mineral are grains, seafood, fresh fish, meat, eggs, onions, and Brazil nuts. A deficiency of boron—which is found in fruits, vegetables, legumes, and nuts—may aggravate the symptoms of arthritis.

red pepper soup

This tasty and colorful soup makes an ideal light appetizer and is delicious topped with crisp whole-wheat croutons. Red bell peppers provide beta carotene and vitamin C; the latter is thought to help joint mobility.

ingredients

- 1tbsp olive oil
- 8 shallots, finely chopped
- 1 large clove garlic, crushed
- 3 large red bell peppers, seeded and diced
- 1¾ cups/1 pound (450g) chopped tomatoes
- 3½ cups/1½ pints (850ml) vegetable stock (see recipe on page 20)
- 2tbsp chopped fresh basil
- sea salt and ground black pepper
- 2tbsp crème fraîche or light sour cream (optional)

serves *four*
preparation time *10 minutes*
cooking time *25–30 minutes*

method

1 Heat the oil in a large saucepan. Add the shallots, garlic, and peppers and cook for 5 minutes.
2 Add the tomatoes and stock. Cover and bring to a boil; then reduce the heat and simmer for 20–25 minutes, until the vegetables are tender.
3 Cool slightly, then purée in a blender or food processor until smooth. Press the mixture through a sieve and discard the pulp.
4 Return the soup to the rinsed-out saucepan. Stir in the chopped basil and seasoning, and reheat gently until piping hot. Stir in the crème fraîche or light sour cream.

5 Ladle into warmed soup bowls, garnish with the basil sprigs, and serve with whole-wheat rolls.

variations

- *Use an onion instead of shallots.*
- *Use a 14-ounce can chopped tomatoes instead of fresh tomatoes.*
- *Use chopped fresh cilantro or parsley instead of basil.*

freezing instructions

Let cool completely, then transfer to a rigid, freezeproof container. Cover, seal, and label. Freeze for up to 3 months. Defrost and reheat gently in a saucepan until piping hot.

soups *and* appetizers

seafood brochettes

These tasty brochettes can be cooked over hot barbecue coals and make a great summertime dish. A deficiency of the trace element selenium, found in seafood, has been linked to rheumatoid arthritis.

ingredients

- 16 shelled tiger shrimp
- 16 scallops
- 8 ounces (225g) salmon fillet, cut into 1-inch (2.5cm) cubes
- 8 ounces (225g) haddock fillet, cut into 1-inch (2.5cm) cubes
- 1 red bell pepper, seeded and cut into 8 pieces
- 1 yellow bell pepper, seeded and cut into 8 pieces
- 16 cherry tomatoes
- 4tbsp olive oil
- finely grated rind and juice of 2 limes
- 1tsp Chinese 5-spice powder
- sea salt
- freshly ground black pepper

serves *four*
preparation time *10 minutes, plus 2–3 hours' marinating time*
cooking time *8–10 minutes*

method

1 Thread the mixed seafood and vegetables onto eight skewers, dividing the ingredients evenly between them. Put the skewers in a shallow, nonmetallic dish.
2 Put the oil, lime rind and juice, spice, and seasoning in a bowl and whisk until thoroughly mixed. Drizzle over the brochettes, then turn the brochettes over in the marinade to coat them completely. Cover and leave to marinate in the refrigerator for 2–3 hours.
3 Preheat the broiler to high. Place the brochettes on a broiler rack in a grill pan and broil for 8–10 minutes, until cooked, turning occasionally. Brush the brochettes frequently with the marinade during cooking.
4 Serve the seafood brochettes with whole-wheat rolls.

variation

- *Use button mushrooms instead of cherry tomatoes.*

green vegetable frittata

Frittatas are quick and easy to make for a tasty and filling appetizer. Green vegetables contain beta carotene and vitamin C as well as boron, which is an important bone mineral.

ingredients

- 6 ounces (175g) small broccoli florets
- 2/3 cup/4 ounces (115g) frozen peas
- 2tbsp olive oil
- 1 onion, chopped
- 1½ cups/8 ounces (225g) diced, cold boiled potatoes
- 1 cup/2 ounces (55g) shredded spinach
- 6 medium eggs
- 2tbsp chopped fresh mixed herbs
- sea salt
- freshly ground black pepper
- ½ cup/2 ounces (55g) grated Cheddar cheese

serves *four to six*
preparation time *10 minutes*
cooking time *25–30 minutes*

method

1 Cook the broccoli and peas in a saucepan of boiling water for 4 minutes. Drain thoroughly.
2 Heat the oil in a large nonstick skillet. Add the onion, and cook gently for 10 minutes.
3 Add the potatoes and spinach, and cook for 5 minutes.
4 Beat the eggs and add the broccoli, peas, herbs, and seasoning. Pour over the vegetables in the pan, spreading evenly.
5 Cook over a medium heat until the eggs are beginning to set and the frittata is brown underneath.
6 Preheat the broiler to medium.
7 Sprinkle the cheese over the top of the frittata and broil until the cheese has melted and the top is golden brown.
8 Cut into wedges and serve hot with a mixed tomato, bell pepper, and onion salad.

variations

- *Use sliced zucchini instead of broccoli florets.*
- *Use 6 shallots instead of the onion.*

pan-fried citrus trout

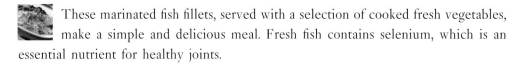 These marinated fish fillets, served with a selection of cooked fresh vegetables, make a simple and delicious meal. Fresh fish contains selenium, which is an essential nutrient for healthy joints.

ingredients

- 8 trout fillets, each weighing 3 ounces (85g)
- pared rind and juice of 1 large lemon
- juice of 1 orange
- 2 cloves garlic, crushed
- sea salt
- freshly ground black pepper
- 1 tbsp olive oil
- 1 tbsp/¹⁄₂ ounce (15g) butter
- 1 tbsp chopped fresh parsley
- 1 tbsp chopped fresh basil

serves *four*
preparation time *10 minutes, plus 1 hour marinating time*
cooking time *10 minutes*

method

1 Put the fish fillets in a shallow, nonmetallic dish.

2 Mix together the lemon rind and juice, orange juice, garlic, and seasoning and pour over the fish. Turn the fish over in the marinade. Cover and leave in the refrigerator to marinate for 1 hour.

3 Heat the oil and butter in a large nonstick skillet until the butter is melted. Using a slotted spoon, remove the fish from the marinade and add to the pan.

4 Cook for 2–3 minutes on each side, until the fish is cooked and the flesh flakes when tested with a fork.

5 Using a fish slice, put the fish on a warmed serving plate, cover, and keep hot.

6 Add the marinade to the pan, discarding the lemon rind. Bring to a boil and boil rapidly for a few minutes, stirring occasionally, until the sauce has reduced and thickened slightly.

7 Pour the sauce over the fish and sprinkle with the fresh herbs. Serve hot with cooked fresh vegetables such as new potatoes, spinach, and baby carrots.

variation

- *Use chopped fresh cilantro instead of basil.*

fish dishes

shrimp *and* broccoli stir-fry

Stir-frying is a quick and easy way of cooking vegetables. The addition of shrimp to this stir-fry makes it extra tasty and nutritious. Broccoli contains carotenoids, vitamin C, and boron, which are all vital nutrients for joint mobility and function.

ingredients

- 8 ounces (225g) small broccoli florets
- 2tsp cornstarch
- 4tbsp unsweetened apple juice
- 1tbsp dry sherry
- 1tbsp light soy sauce
- 1tbsp honey
- 2tsp tomato paste
- salt
- freshly ground black pepper
- 1tbsp olive oil
- 1 clove garlic, finely chopped
- 1-inch (2.5cm) piece fresh ginger root, peeled and finely chopped
- 1 carrot, cut into matchstick (julienne) strips
- 2 zucchini, cut into matchstick (julienne) strips
- 12 ounces (350g) cooked, shelled shrimp
- 4 ounces (115g) bean sprouts

serves *four to six*
preparation time *15 minutes*
cooking time *8–10 minutes*

method

1 Cook the broccoli in a saucepan of boiling water for 2 minutes. Drain thoroughly and keep warm.

2 In a small bowl, blend the cornstarch with the apple juice. Stir in the sherry, soy sauce, honey, tomato paste, and seasoning. Set aside.

3 Heat the oil in a nonstick wok or large skillet. Add the garlic and ginger, and stir-fry over a high heat for 30 seconds. Add the carrot and zucchini and stir-fry for 2–3 minutes.

4 Add the broccoli, shrimp, and bean sprouts, and stir-fry for another 2–3 minutes. Add the cornstarch mixture and stir-fry until the mixture thickens; then stir-fry for another 1–2 minutes.

5 Serve with brown and wild rice.

variations

- *Use cauliflower florets instead of broccoli.*

fish *dishes*

braised chicken livers *with* fresh thyme

 Tender chicken livers combined with fresh wild mushrooms and thyme make a tasty and nutritious dish. Liver provides vitamin A and selenium, an antioxidant that is important for joints. The olive oil used for frying provides omega-6 fatty acids, which aid joint mobility.

ingredients

- 2tbsp olive oil
- 1 large onion, sliced
- 1 pound (450g) chicken livers, thinly sliced
- 6 ounces (175g) mixed fresh wild mushrooms, such as shiitake and oyster, sliced
- 12 ounces (350g) tomatoes, peeled, seeded, and cut into thin strips
- ⅔ cup/¼ pint (150ml) red wine or dry white wine
- 1tbsp chopped fresh thyme
- sea salt
- freshly ground black pepper
- fresh thyme sprigs, to garnish

serves *four to six*
preparation time *15 minutes*
cooking time *8–10 minutes*

method

1 Heat the oil in a large nonstick skillet, add the onion, and cook gently for 10 minutes, stirring occasionally, until softened.

2 Add the chicken livers and mushrooms. Cook for 5 minutes, stirring.

3 Add the tomatoes, wine, and chopped thyme. Bring to a boil and simmer for another 5 minutes until the liver is cooked, stirring occasionally.

4 Season to taste.

5 Serve hot, garnished with fresh thyme sprigs, with potatoes and braised carrots and celery.

variations

· *Use stock instead of wine.*

· *Use a red onion instead of a regular onion.*

meat and poultry dishes

oven-baked turkey *with* mango salsa

Oven-baked succulent turkey cutlets served with a fruity salsa are sure to make this a family favorite. The mangoes used in the salsa are a good source of carotenoids and vitamin C, both of which are vital for joint mobility and function.

ingredients

- 4 skinless, boneless turkey cutlets
- 1 tbsp olive oil
- 2 tbsp whole-grain mustard
- 2 tbsp chopped fresh tarragon
- sea salt
- freshly ground black pepper
- 1 onion, thinly sliced
- juice of 1 large lemon
- fresh herb sprigs, to garnish

for the salsa

- 1 large mango, peeled, pitted, and finely chopped
- ⅓ cup/2 ounces (55g) finely chopped, English cucumber
- 4 green onions, finely chopped
- 1 tbsp chopped fresh cilantro

serves *four*
preparation time *15 minutes, plus 1–2 hours' standing time*
cooking time *30–45 minutes*

method

1 First make the salsa. Put the mango, cucumber, green onions, and cilantro in a bowl and mix thoroughly. Cover and leave to stand at room temperature for 1–2 hours.

2 Preheat the oven to 375°F. Cut four pieces of greaseproof paper, each large enough to hold a turkey cutlet in a package. Cut three slashes in each turkey cutlet and place on the paper.

3 Mix together the oil, mustard, tarragon, and seasoning in a small bowl. Spread some of the mixture over each turkey cutlet.

4 Place a few slices of onion on top of each turkey cutlet, then drizzle lemon juice over the top. Fold the paper over the turkey cutlets and twist the edges to secure, making four packages.

5 Place the packages on a baking tray and bake for 30–45 minutes, until the turkey is cooked and tender.

6 Undo the packages carefully (to avoid getting burned by steam) and place the cooked turkey on warmed serving plates. Spoon the juices over the turkey and spoon the salsa alongside. Garnish with fresh herb sprigs.

7 Serve with sautéed potatoes and broiled bell peppers.

variations

- *Use skinless, boneless chicken breasts instead of turkey.*
- *Use a small fresh pineapple instead of a mango.*
- *Use chopped fresh cilantro or basil instead of tarragon.*

summer vegetable quiche

This tasty quiche makes an ideal summertime lunch or snack. It contains green vegetables such as broccoli and asparagus, which provide boron, a trace element that is good for bones and joints.

ingredients

for the pastry

- 1½ cups/6 ounces (175g) whole-wheat flour
- dash of salt
- ⅓ cup/3 ounces (85g) butter

for the filling

- 2 ounces (55g) small broccoli florets
- 2 ounces (55g) asparagus tips
- 1 zucchini, thinly sliced
- 2 plum (Roma) tomatoes, sliced
- ¾ cup/3 ounces (85g) grated Cheddar cheese
- 2 medium-sized eggs
- ⅔ cup/¼ pint (150ml) milk
- 1–2tbsp chopped fresh mixed herbs
- sea salt
- freshly ground black pepper

serves *six*
preparation time *15 minutes, plus chilling time*
cooking time *55 minutes*

method

1 Put the flour and salt into a bowl, then lightly rub in the butter until the mixture resembles bread crumbs. Stir in enough cold water to form a soft dough.
2 Roll the dough out and line an 8-inch pie pan. Cover and chill for 20 minutes.
3 Preheat the oven to 400°F.
4 Line the pastry shell with nonstick baking paper and fill with baking beans. Place on a baking tray and bake blind in the oven for 10 minutes. Remove from the oven and reduce the oven temperature to 350°F.
5 Blanch the broccoli, asparagus, and zucchini in boiling water for 2 minutes. Drain and spoon into the pastry shell. Top with the tomato slices and sprinkle with the cheese.
6 Beat the eggs, milk, herbs, and seasoning, and pour into the pastry shell. Bake for about 45 minutes, until golden brown.
7 Serve warm or cold in slices, with baked potatoes and a salad.

bean *and* vegetable chili

A delicious alternative to meat, this nutritious bean and vegetable chili, served with brown rice, is ideal for cold days. Fresh vegetables provide carotenoids, vitamin C, and selenium.

ingredients

- 1tbsp olive oil
- 1 onion, sliced
- 1 red bell pepper, seeded and diced
- 2 fresh red chilies, seeded and finely chopped
- 2 cloves garlic, finely chopped
- 2tsp ground coriander
- 2 carrots, sliced
- 8 ounces (225g) cauliflower florets
- 1 14-ounce (400g) can chopped tomatoes
- 1¼ cups/½ pint (300ml) vegetable stock
- 2tbsp sun-dried tomato paste
- sea salt
- freshly ground black pepper
- 14-ounce (400g) can each red kidney beans and green haricot beans, rinsed and drained
- 2tbsp cornstarch
- fresh cilantro sprigs, to garnish

serves *four to six*
preparation time *20 minutes*
cooking time *40–45 minutes*

method

1 Heat the oil in a large saucepan. Add the onion, pepper, chilies, garlic, and coriander, and cook gently for 5 minutes.
2 Add the carrots, cauliflower, tomatoes, stock, tomato paste, and seasoning, and stir. Cover and bring to a boil; then reduce the heat and simmer for 25 minutes.
3 Stir in the beans. Bring back to a boil and cook for another 10–15 minutes, until the vegetables are tender.
4 Blend the cornstarch with 4tbsp water and stir into the bean mixture. Bring to a boil, stirring continuously, until the mixture thickens slightly. Simmer for 2 minutes, stirring.
5 Serve on a bed of brown rice, pasta, or couscous, and garnish with fresh cilantro sprigs.

variations

- Use other canned legumes, such as black-eyed peas or lima beans.
- Use broccoli florets instead of cauliflower florets.

cherry buckwheat pancakes

 These buckwheat pancakes make an appealing dessert served with a delicious, sweet cherry sauce. Red fruits such as cherries contain carotenoids and vitamin C.

ingredients

for the sauce

- ½ cup/4 fluid ounces (125ml) red wine
- ¼ cup/2 ounces (55g) light brown sugar
- 8 ounces (225g) pitted fresh sweet dark cherries
- 2tsp arrowroot
- 2tbsp cherry brandy

for the pancakes

- ½ cup/2 ounces (55g) whole-wheat flour
- ½ cup/2 ounces (55g) buckwheat flour
- dash of salt
- 1 medium-sized egg
- 1¼ cups/½ pint (300ml) milk
- sunflower oil, for frying

serves *four (two pancakes each)*
preparation time *25 minutes*
cooking time *15–20 minutes*

method

1 Put the red wine and sugar in a saucepan and heat gently until the sugar has dissolved, stirring continuously. Add the cherries, cover, and bring to a boil. Reduce the heat and cook gently for 10 minutes until the cherries are tender, stirring occasionally.

2 Blend the arrowroot with the cherry brandy and stir it into the cherry mixture. Bring to a boil, stirring continuously until the mixture thickens. Keep the sauce warm while making the pancakes, or serve it cold.

3 To make the pancakes, put the whole-wheat flour, buckwheat flour, and salt in a bowl, and make a well in the center. Break in the egg and add a little milk, beating well with a wooden spoon.

4 Gradually beat in the remaining milk, drawing the flour in from the sides, to make a smooth batter.

5 Heat a little oil in a 7-inch nonstick skillet. Pour in enough batter to coat the base of the pan thinly. Cook until golden brown; then turn and cook on the other side.

6 Transfer the cooked pancake to a warmed plate and keep hot. Repeat with the remaining batter to make eight pancakes, stacking them in layers between nonstick paper.

7 Serve the hot pancakes with warm or cold cherry sauce poured over. Add a little crème fraîche, light sour cream, or yogurt, if desired.

variations

- *Use unsweetened apple juice instead of cherry brandy.*
- *Use plums or raspberries instead of cherries.*
- *Use all whole-wheat flour.*

freezing instructions

To freeze the pancakes, beat 1tbsp sunflower oil into the basic recipe, then cook as directed, and let cool. Interleave the cooked pancakes with lightly oiled nonstick paper or freezer-wrap. Seal in polythene freezer bags or foil and freeze for up to 2 months. Defrost and reheat each pancake separately in a lightly greased skillet, about 30 seconds for each side.

mixed berry yogurt fool

 This tasty fruit fool is quick and easy to make. Berries contain carotenoids and vitamin C, vital nutrients for joint mobility and function.

■ ingredients

- 1½ pounds (700g) fresh ripe mixed berries, such as strawberries, raspberries, and blackberries
- 4tbsp honey
- 1¼ cups/10 ounces plain yogurt
- 6tbsp crème fraîche or light sour cream
- fresh mint sprigs, to decorate

serves *six*
preparation time *15 minutes, plus 30 minutes' chilling time*

■ method

1 Put the mixed berries in a blender or food processor and blend until smooth. Press the purée through a sieve into a bowl, reserving the juice and pulp and discarding the seeds.

2 Mix the honey with the fruit. Stir the yogurt and crème fraîche or light sour cream into the fruit mixture until thoroughly mixed.

3 Spoon into serving glasses or dishes and chill for 30 minutes before serving. Decorate with fresh mint sprigs and serve with homemade oat cookies.

variations

• For a mango yogurt fool, replace the mixed berries with the same quantity of peeled, pitted, ripe mango flesh.

• This fruit fool can be set with gelatin. Follow the recipe as directed, and before chilling dissolve 1tbsp powdered gelatin in 3tbsp water. Cool slightly, then stir into the berry mixture, mixing thoroughly. Pour into serving glasses and chill until set.

marbled cheesecake

This delicious, fruity cheesecake is a real treat for dessert. Blackcurrants are an excellent source of vitamin C and potassium.

■ ingredients

- 1½ cups/6 ounces (175g) frozen blackcurrants, cherries, or raspberries, defrosted
- ⅓–½ cup/3½ ounces (100g) light brown sugar
- ⅓ cup/3 ounces (85g) butter
- 1¾ cups/6 ounces (175g) muesli or granola
- 1tbsp powdered gelatin
- ½ cup/4 ounces (115g) cottage cheese, drained
- ½ cup/4 ounces (115g) plain yogurt, drained
- ⅔ cup/¼ pint (150ml) light cream
- finely grated rind and juice of 1 lemon
- small bunches of redcurrants and fresh mint sprigs, to decorate

serves *six to eight*
preparation time *25 minutes, plus chilling time*

■ method

1 Purée the fruit and 3tbsp sugar in a food processor. Press through a sieve.

2 Melt the butter in a saucepan. Remove from the heat and stir in the muesli. Press the mixture over the bottom of an 8-inch springform cake pan. Chill for 30 minutes.

3 Sprinkle the gelatin over 3tbsp water in a small bowl. Soak for a couple of minutes, then place over a pan of simmering water, and stir until dissolved.

4 Place the remaining sugar, cheese, yogurt, cream, lemon rind, and juice in a food processor and blend. Add the gelatin and blend until well mixed. Pour into the pan over the muesli base.

5 Pour the fruit purée in a thin stream over the cheese mixture and swirl the two mixtures to create a marbled effect. Refrigerate until set.

6 Remove from the pan, decorate with mint sprigs, and serve in slices.

desserts *and* bakes

a *moveable* feast

THESE DELICIOUS RECIPES *from the flexibility foods section help supply the vitamins and minerals necessary to ensure* that the joints are well oiled and functioning properly. So *have your knife and fork ready to keep mobile and help to prevent osteoporosis and arthritis.*

red pepper soup

Kick off with red peppers for a good dose of beta carotene and vitamin C—vital nutrients for joint mobility and function.

■ ingredients

- 1tbsp olive oil
- 8 shallots, finely chopped
- 1 large clove garlic, crushed
- 3 large red bell peppers, seeded and diced
- 1³/₄ cups/1 pound (450g) chopped tomatoes
- 3¹/₂ cups/1¹/₂ pints (850ml) vegetable stock (see recipe on page 20)
- 2tbsp chopped fresh basil
- sea salt and ground black pepper
- 2tbsp crème fraîche or light sour cream (optional)

serves *four*
preparation time *10 minutes*
cooking time *25–30 minutes*

■ method

1 Heat the oil in a large pan. Add the shallots, garlic, and peppers and cook for 5 minutes.
2 Add the tomatoes and stock. Cover and bring to a boil; then reduce the heat and simmer for 20–25 minutes, until the vegetables are tender.
3 Cool slightly, then purée in a blender or food processor until smooth. Press the mixture through a sieve and discard the pulp.
4 Return the soup to the rinsed-out pan. Stir in the chopped basil and seasoning, and reheat gently until piping hot. Stir in the crème fraîche or light sour cream.
5 Ladle into warmed soup bowls, garnish with the basil sprigs, and serve with whole-wheat rolls.

oven-baked turkey *with* mango salsa

To complement zinc-rich turkey, the mangoes in the salsa are another good source of joint-boosters vitamin C and carotenoids.

■ ingredients

- 4 skinless, boneless turkey cutlets
- 1tbsp olive oil
- 2tbsp whole-grain mustard
- 2tbsp chopped fresh tarragon
- sea salt
- freshly ground black pepper
- 1 onion, thinly sliced
- juice of 1 large lemon
- fresh herb sprigs, to garnish

for the salsa

- 1 large mango, peeled, pitted, and finely chopped
- ¹/₃ cup/2 ounces (55g) finely chopped, English cucumber
- 4 green onions, finely chopped
- 1tbsp chopped fresh cilantro

serves *four*
preparation time *15 minutes, plus 1–2 hours' standing time*
cooking time *30–45 minutes*

method

1 First make the salsa. Put the mango, cucumber, green onions, and cilantro in a bowl and mix thoroughly. Cover and leave to stand at room temperature for 1–2 hours.

2 Preheat the oven to 375°F. Cut four pieces of greaseproof paper, each large enough to hold a turkey cutlet in a package. Cut three slashes in each turkey cutlet and place each one on the paper.

3 Mix together the oil, mustard, tarragon, and seasoning in a small bowl. Spread some of the mixture over each turkey cutlet.

4 Place a few slices of onion on top of each turkey cutlet, then drizzle lemon juice over the top. Fold the paper over the turkey cutlets and twist the edges to secure, making four packages.

5 Place the packages on a baking tray and bake for 30–45 minutes, until the turkey is cooked and tender.

6 Undo the packages carefully (to avoid getting burned by steam) and place the cooked turkey on warmed serving plates. Spoon the juices over the turkey and spoon the salsa alongside. Garnish with fresh herb sprigs.

7 Serve with sautéed potatoes and broiled bell peppers.

marbled cheesecake

This delicious fruity cheesecake is a real treat for dessert. Blackcurrants are an excellent source of potassium and vitamin C.

ingredients

- 1½ cups/6 ounces (175g) frozen blackcurrants, cherries, or raspberries, defrosted
- ⅓–½ cup/3½ ounces (100g) light brown sugar
- ⅓ cup/3 ounces (85g) butter
- 1¾ cups/6 ounces (175g) muesli or granola
- 1 tbsp powdered gelatin
- ½ cup/4 ounces (115g) cottage cheese, drained
- ½ cup/4 ounces (115g) plain yogurt, drained
- ⅔ cup/¼ pint (150ml) light cream
- finely grated rind and juice of 1 lemon
- small bunches of redcurrants and fresh mint sprigs, to decorate

serves *six to eight*
preparation time *25 minutes*

method

1 Purée the fruit and 3tbsp sugar in a food processor. Press through a sieve.

2 Melt the butter in a saucepan. Remove from the heat and stir in the muesli. Press the mixture over the bottom of an 8-inch springform cake pan. Chill for 30 minutes.

3 Sprinkle the gelatin over 3tbsp water in a small bowl. Soak for a couple of minutes, then place over a pan of simmering water, and stir until dissolved.

4 Place the remaining sugar, cheese, yogurt, cream, lemon rind, and juice in a food processor and blend. Add the gelatin and blend until well mixed. Pour into the pan over the muesli base.

5 Pour the fruit purée in a thin stream over the cheese mixture and swirl the two mixtures to create a marbled effect. Refrigerate until set.

6 Remove from the pan, decorate with mint sprigs, and serve in slices.

beauty

For the Beauty section, we have devised recipes to help maintain your health and reshape your body, and have also suggested numerous foods which help improve your skin, nails, hair, and eyes.

We have included plenty of fruits and vegetables such as lemons, artichokes, dandelion, apples, pineapple, and grapefruit, which are not only rich in fiber, but also contain compounds that help the body deal with potentially toxic substances. The recipes are low in fat to help reduce calories. Of course, coupling these recipes with exercise is the ideal way to derive full benefit.

Healthy skin requires a good supply of vitamin A, some of which our body synthesizes from beta carotene, a plant source of vitamin A. Carrots, tomatoes, cantaloupe, spinach, sweet potatoes, and apricots

FOODS

are great sources. Oily fish, walnuts, flaxseeds, sunflower, and pumpkin seeds and their oils, are rich in essential fats and vitamin E, which also play a role in maintaining healthy skin. The B vitamins, along with iron and zinc, are important for healthy skin, hair, and nails, and can be found in brown rice, oats, sardines, wheat germ, Brewer's yeast, pumpkin seeds, raisins, broccoli, peas, and sweet potatoes.

For optimum health, your eyes need vitamins A and B as well as essential fatty acids. Excellent sources are liver (for vitamins A and B), oily fish (for vitamin B_{12} and essential fatty acids), and carrots, spinach, broccoli, and apricots (for vitamin A derived from beta carotene). Blueberries and blackberries contain flavonoids, which act as antioxidants and help to strengthen the small capillaries and lower the risk of cataracts. Our recipes are rich in all these foods – we hope you enjoy them.

light *eating*

I T IS A *nutritional fact that maintaining a well-balanced diet is vital for optimal health. However, after overindulging in food, perhaps during a vacation, you may feel like eating lighter meals for a day. Good foods to include in a lighter meal regimen are fresh fruits and vegetables, yogurt, and brown rice. Foods to* avoid *are fatty meats and salty snacks. The types of liquids you drink, and how much of them you drink, is as important as the foods you eat. Plenty of water, low-fat milk, and unsweetened fruit juices are the most beneficial; caffeinated beverages such as coffee, colas, and teas, and alcohol should be avoided.*

mango *and* apricot smoothie

 This naturally sweet fruit drink is an excellent light and refreshing beverage. Mangoes and apricots are rich in vitamin C and other antioxidants.

ingredients

- I large ripe mango
- 8 ripe apricots

serves *two*
(makes 1³/₄ cups/³/₄ pint/425ml)
preparation time *10 minutes*

method

1 Peel and pit the mango and roughly chop the flesh. Halve and pit the apricots.
2 Place the mango flesh and apricots in a blender or food processor with ³/₄ cup water and blend until smooth.
3 Press the mixture through a sieve and discard the pulp.
4 Pour the juice into glasses and serve immediately, or cover and chill before serving.

variations

- *Use I small pineapple instead of the mango.*
- *Use freshly squeezed orange juice instead of water.*

drinks

banana yogurt shake

This creamy banana yogurt shake can be whizzed up in no time at all. Bananas are packed full of nutrients, including potassium, magnesium, vitamin B$_6$, and vitamin C.

ingredients

- 1¼ cups/½ pint (300ml) plain yogurt
- 2 bananas, peeled and sliced

serves *two*
(makes 2¼ cups/18 fluid ounces/500ml)
preparation time *5 minutes*

method

1. Put the yogurt and bananas in a blender or food processor and blend until smooth.
2. Pour into glasses and serve immediately.

variation

- *Use other fruits, such as 8 ounces (225g) strawberries or peaches, instead of bananas.*

drinks

vitamin C drink

This refreshing drink, with its sharp, fruity flavor, makes a great start to the day. Vitamin C is an antioxidant that is important in numerous body functions.

ingredients

- 1 pink grapefruit
- 1 orange
- 2 kiwi fruit
- 4 ounces (115g) strawberries

serves *two*
(makes 1³/₄ cups/¹/₂ pint/425 ml)
preparation time *10 minutes*

method

1 Peel the grapefruit and orange, removing as much pith as possible; then break the fruit into segments. Peel and quarter the kiwi fruit.

2 Place the grapefruit and orange segments, kiwi fruit, and strawberries in a blender or food processor and blend until smooth.

3 Press the mixture through a sieve and discard the pulp.

4 Pour the juice into glasses and serve immediately, or cover and chill before serving.

variations

- *Use raspberries instead of strawberries.*
- *Use 2 or 3 satsumas or clementines instead of the orange.*

drinks

chunky vegetable soup

Chunky vegetables cooked with herbs in homemade stock make a tasty, warming soup that is excellent for a healthy diet. Carrots, turnips, potatoes, and parsnips add antioxidants galore.

▌ ingredients

- 1 large onion, finely chopped
- 2 celery stalks, chopped
- 8 ounces (225g) carrots, thinly sliced
- 1½ cups/8 ounces (225g) diced parsnips
- 1¼ cups/6 ounces (175g) diced potatoes or celeriac
- 1¼ cups/6 ounces (175g) diced turnip
- 3½ cups/1½ pints (850ml) vegetable stock (see recipe on page 20)
- 2tsp dried *herbes de provence*
- sea salt
- freshly ground black pepper
- fresh herb sprigs, to garnish

serves *four*
preparation time *15 minutes*
cooking time *25 minutes*

▌ method

1 Put all the vegetables into a pan with the stock, dried herbs, and seasoning, and stir.

2 Cover and bring to a boil; then reduce the heat and simmer for about 25 minutes, until the vegetables are cooked and tender, stirring occasionally.

3 Ladle into warmed soup bowls and garnish with fresh herb sprigs.

variations

• *This soup may be puréed in a blender or food processor before serving, if preferred. Reheat gently until piping hot, before serving.*
• *Use 2 leeks instead of the onion.*
• *Use rutabaga and sweet potatoes instead of the turnip and parsnips.*

freezing instructions

Let cool completely, then transfer to a rigid, freezeproof container. Cover, seal, and label. Freeze for up to 3 months. Defrost and reheat gently in a pan until piping hot.

soups

fresh pea *and* onion soup *with* parsley

 This tasty mixture of fresh vegetables makes a light, nutritious soup. Fresh parsley is more than a garnish—it's a good source of vitamin C.

ingredients

- 1 tbsp olive oil
- 1 onion, finely chopped
- 2 leeks, washed and sliced
- 2½ cups/12 ounces (350g) diced potatoes
- 1¼ cups/8 ounces (225g) fresh shelled peas
- 3½ cups/1½ pints (850ml) vegetable stock (see recipe on page 20)
- sea salt
- freshly ground black pepper
- 2 tbsp chopped fresh parsley
- fresh parsley sprigs, to garnish

serves *four to six*
preparation time *15 minutes*
cooking time *20–25 minutes*

method

1 Heat the oil in a large pan. Add the onion and leeks, and cook gently for 3 minutes, stirring.
2 Add the potatoes, peas, stock, and seasoning, and stir. Cover and bring to a boil; then reduce the heat and simmer for 15–20 minutes, stirring occasionally, until the vegetables are tender.
3 Remove the pan from the heat and set aside to cool slightly; then purée the soup in a blender or food processor until smooth.
4 Return the soup to the rinsed-out pan. Add the chopped parsley and reheat gently until piping hot, stirring occasionally.
5 Ladle into warmed soup bowls and garnish with parsley sprigs.

variations

- The soup does not have to be puréed before serving, and the vegetables can be left in small pieces, if preferred.
- Use sweet potatoes instead of potatoes.
- Use chopped fresh tarragon instead of parsley.

freezing instructions

Let cool completely, then transfer to a rigid, freezeproof container. Cover, seal, and label. Freeze for up to 3 months. Defrost and reheat gently in a pan until piping hot.

chilled cucumber *and* mint soup

This delicious chilled soup makes a refreshing change. Garlic can lower cholesterol and blood pressure and also has anti-bacterial and anti-fungal properties. Yogurt provides easily digestible protein, while cucumbers are low in calories.

ingredients

- 1 English cucumber, seeded and diced
- 3 shallots, chopped
- 1 large clove garlic, crushed
- ²/₃ cup/¹/₄ pint (150ml) cold vegetable stock (see recipe on page 20)
- 2 cups/¹/₂ pint (300ml) plain yogurt
- 1 cup/¹/₄ pint (150ml) low-fat plain yogurt
- 2–3tbsp chopped fresh mint
- sea salt
- freshly ground black pepper
- fresh mint sprigs, to garnish

serves *four*
preparation time *10 minutes,
plus chilling time*

method

1 Put the cucumber, shallots, garlic, and stock in a blender or food processor, and blend until smooth.

2 Add the yogurt and blend until relatively smooth. Pour the mixture into a bowl.

3 Stir in the chopped mint and season well with salt and pepper.

4 Cover and refrigerate for at least 1 hour before serving.

5 Ladle into soup bowls and serve garnished with fresh mint sprigs.

variations

- *Use chopped fresh tarragon or cilantro instead of mint.*
- *Use 1 small onion instead of shallots.*

soups

char-broiled vegetable salad

 Broiled vegetables make a tasty appetizer or main dish and are excellent for light-eating days. Dandelion leaves give a vitamin boost to salads and are a natural diuretic.

ingredients

- 8 shallots, thinly sliced
- 2 zucchini, halved and then thinly sliced lengthways
- 2 red bell peppers, seeded and sliced
- 1 small eggplant, thinly sliced
- 4 plum (Roma) tomatoes, halved
- 4 ounces (115g) mixed dark-green salad leaves such as spinach, young dandelion leaves, and watercress
- 2tbsp chopped fresh parsley

for the dressing

- 3tbsp olive oil
- juice of 1 lemon
- sea salt
- freshly ground black pepper

serves *four to six*
preparation time *10 minutes*
cooking time *8–10 minutes*

method

1 Preheat the broiler to high. Line the broiler rack with foil. Put the shallots, zucchini, peppers, eggplants, and tomatoes on the prepared broiler rack.

2 In a small bowl, whisk together the oil, lemon juice, and seasoning. Lightly brush the vegetables with some of the oil mixture and broil them for 8–10 minutes, until cooked and tender. Turn and brush lightly with the oil mixture halfway through the cooking time.

2 Divide the salad leaves between four serving plates. Spoon the hot broiled vegetables onto the salad leaves and sprinkle some parsley over the top of each portion.

3 Serve immediately with a glass of freshly squeezed orange juice.

variations

- *Drizzle a little French dressing (see recipe on page 21) over the hot broiled vegetables just before serving.*
- *Use regular red or yellow tomatoes instead of plum tomatoes.*
- *Use the juice of a lime instead of a lemon.*
- *Use chopped fresh mixed herbs or chives instead of parsley.*

salads

exotic dried fruit compote

This simple compote of dried fruits and fruit juices is easy to make and delicious to eat. It is a great light snack or dessert.

■ ingredients

- 2¹/₂ cups/12 ounces (350g) mixed exotic dried fruit including mango, figs, pineapple, apricots, and peaches
- ³/₄ cup/7 fluid ounces (200ml) unsweetened apple or grape juice
- ³/₄ cup/7 fluid ounces (200ml) unsweetened orange juice

serves *four*
preparation time *5 minutes, plus 4 hours' standing time*

■ method

1 Put the dried fruit in a serving bowl. Add the apple or grape juice, and orange juice. Stir.
2 Cover and chill in the refrigerator overnight.
3 Serve with plain yogurt.

variations

• *This fruit salad may be served warm. After standing overnight in the refrigerator, put the fruit and juices in a pan and bring gently to a boil. Remove the pan from the heat and set aside to cool slightly, then serve warm.*
• *The fruit may be chopped before soaking in the fruit juices.*

five-fruit salad

Fresh fruits are important for a healthy circulatory system and digestive tract. They are filled with antioxidants as well as soluble and insoluble fiber.

■ ingredients

- 1¹/₄ cups/¹/₂ pint (300ml) unsweetened grape juice
- 1¹/₄ cups/¹/₂ pint (300ml) unsweetened orange juice
- 1 small melon
- 2 ripe peaches
- 2 eating apples
- 4 ounces (115g) green seedless grapes
- 1¹/₂ cups/6 ounces (175g) fresh raspberries
- fresh mint sprigs, to decorate

serves *six*
preparation time *15 minutes, plus 2–3 hours' standing time*

■ method

1 Put the grape and orange juices in a serving bowl and stir.
2 Peel and seed the melon and dice the flesh. Peel and pit the peaches and chop the flesh. Add the melon and peaches to the fruit juices.
3 Peel, core, and slice or chop the apple and add to the fruit juices with the grapes and raspberries. Stir gently.
4 Cover and refrigerate for 2–3 hours before serving, to let the flavors blend.
5 Decorate with fresh mint sprigs and serve with plain yogurt.

variations

• *Use a small pineapple instead of the melon.*
• *Use nectarines instead of peaches.*
• *Use pears and strawberries instead of apples and raspberries.*

shape *foods*

A HEALTHY DIET *includes plenty of vegetables and fruit, as well as the complex carbohydrates— bread, cereals, potatoes, legumes, and pasta—and moderate amounts of low-fat dairy foods, eggs, chicken, fish and lean meat. By eating a variety of foods in sensible proportions you can obtain all the nutrients you need.*

Italian chicken casserole

 Chicken portions are braised with vegetables to make this flavorsome dish. Cooked without the skin, chicken is an excellent protein food, low in saturated fat.

▌ ingredients

- 1 tbsp olive oil
- 4 skinless chicken cutlets
- 12 ounces (350g) pearl onions
- 1 clove garlic, crushed
- 1 red bell pepper, seeded and diced
- 8 ounces (225g) button mushrooms
- 1 14-ounce (400g) can chopped tomatoes
- ²/₃ cup/¹/₄ pint (150ml) chicken stock (see recipe on page 20)
- ³/₄ cup/¹/₄ pint (150ml) red wine
- 1 tbsp chopped fresh thyme
- 1 tbsp chopped fresh oregano
- sea salt
- freshly ground black pepper
- fresh herb sprigs, to garnish

serves *four*
preparation time *15 minutes*
cooking time *1½ hours*

▌ method

1 Preheat the oven to 350°F.
2 Heat the oil in a flameproof, ovenproof casserole. Add the chicken and cook until sealed all over, turning occasionally.
3 Add all the remaining ingredients, except the herb garnish, and stir. Bring to a boil, stirring occasionally.
4 Cover and bake for about 1 hour, until the chicken and vegetables are cooked and tender, stirring once or twice.
5 Remove the cooked chicken and vegetables from the casserole using a slotted spoon, place on warmed plates, and keep hot.

6 Bring the sauce to a boil and boil rapidly for a few minutes until it has reduced and thickened. Spoon the sauce over the chicken and vegetables.
7 Garnish with fresh herb sprigs.
8 Serve with cooked fresh vegetables such as broccoli and cauliflower florets.

variations

- *Use small turkey cutlets instead of chicken.*
- *Use shallots instead of pearl onions.*
- *Use white wine or unsweetened apple juice instead of red wine.*

freezing instructions

Let cool completely, then transfer to a rigid, freezeproof container. Cover, seal, and label. Freeze for up to 3 months. Defrost completely and reheat in a moderate oven until piping hot.

protein-based *meals*

haddock provençale

These oven-baked haddock fillets are served with a good portion of delicious vegetable sauce. Fish is a complete protein and is rich in selenium, magnesium, and omega-3 essential fatty acids.

ingredients

- 1 onion, sliced
- 1 clove garlic, crushed
- 1 red bell pepper, seeded and sliced
- 1 yellow bell pepper, seeded and sliced
- 2 zucchini, sliced
- 1 14-ounce (400g) can chopped tomatoes
- sea salt
- freshly ground black pepper
- 4 haddock fillets, each weighing about 6 ounces (175g)
- juice of 1 large lemon
- 2tbsp chopped fresh parsley
- 2tbsp chopped fresh basil
- 1/2 cup/2 ounces (55g) black olives
- fresh herb sprigs, to garnish

serves *four*
preparation time *10 minutes*
cooking time *20 minutes*

method

1 Preheat the oven to 350°F.
2 Put the onion, garlic, peppers, zucchini, tomatoes, and seasoning in a pan and stir. Cover and bring to a boil; then reduce the heat and simmer for about 20 minutes, until the vegetables are tender, stirring occasionally.
3 Meanwhile, place the fish fillets in a shallow ovenproof dish. Drizzle the lemon juice over the fish and sprinkle the parsley on top. Cover and bake for 15–20 minutes, until the fish is cooked and the flesh flakes when tested with a fork.
4 Stir the chopped basil into the vegetable sauce.

5 Put the baked haddock fillets on warmed serving plates, spoon some vegetable sauce over each one, and scatter the olives on top. Garnish with the herb sprigs.
6 Serve hot with cooked fresh vegetables such as green beans and baby corn.

variations

- *Use any firm white fish fillets.*
- *Use the juice of 2 limes instead of a lemon.*
- *Use 1 eggplant instead of zucchini.*

protein-based *meals*

broiled lamb cutlets
with plum tomato salsa

 Lamb cutlets broiled and served with a tasty tomato salsa, make an appetizing dish. Tomatoes are particularly rich in vitamin C, lycopene, and other carotenoids, as well as dietary fiber. These nutrients are believed to protect the body against cancer.

ingredients

- 3 cups/1½ pounds (700g) peeled, seeded, and finely chopped plum tomatoes
- 2 green onions, chopped
- 1 large clove garlic, crushed
- 1 tbsp olive oil
- 1 tbsp sun-dried tomato paste
- 1–2 tsp balsamic vinegar
- 2 tbsp chopped fresh basil
- sea salt
- freshly ground black pepper
- 8 lean lamb cutlets

serves *four*
preparation time *15 minutes, plus 1 hour standing time*
cooking time *8–12 minutes*

method

1 Put the tomatoes, green onions, garlic, oil, tomato paste, vinegar, basil, and seasoning in a bowl and mix well. Cover and leave at room temperature for about 1 hour, to let the flavors blend.

2 Preheat the broiler to high. Place the lamb cutlets on a broiler rack in a broiler pan. Broil for 4–6 minutes on each side, until cooked.

3 Place the hot lamb cutlets on serving plates with the tomato salsa spooned alongside.

4 Serve with cooked fresh vegetables such as new potatoes, peas, and baby carrots.

variations

- Use 2 shallots instead of green onions.
- Use chopped fresh chives or cilantro instead of basil.
- Serve the tomato salsa with other broiled lean meats such as chicken or turkey cutlets.

protein-based *meals*

tuna steaks baked *with* spices

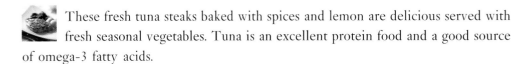

These fresh tuna steaks baked with spices and lemon are delicious served with fresh seasonal vegetables. Tuna is an excellent protein food and a good source of omega-3 fatty acids.

■ ingredients

- 4 tuna steaks, each weighing about 6 ounces (175g)
- 2tsp coriander seeds
- 2tsp cumin seeds
- 1tsp dried crushed chilies
- 1tsp black peppercorns
- sea salt
- finely grated rind and juice of 1 large lemon

serves *four*
preparation time *10 minutes*
cooking time *20 minutes*

■ method

1 Preheat the oven to 375°F.

2 Cut four pieces of nonstick baking paper, each large enough to hold one tuna steak in a package easily. Place a tuna steak on each piece of paper.

3 Put the seeds, crushed chilies, peppercorns, and salt in a mortar. Using a pestle, crush the spices to break them up a little. Stir in the lemon rind.

4 Scatter the spice mixture evenly over the fish steaks, then drizzle a little lemon juice over each one. Fold the paper over the fish and twist the edges to secure, making four packages.

5 Transfer the packages to a baking tray and bake for about 20 minutes, until the fish is cooked and the flesh flakes when tested with a fork.

6 Place the unopened package on a warmed serving plate and serve immediately with cooked fresh vegetables such as new potatoes, baby corn, and carrots.

variations

- *Use salmon steaks instead of tuna.*
- *Use 1 large lime or 1 small orange instead of the lemon.*
- *Use mixed peppercorns instead of black peppercorns.*

protein-based *meals*

herbed rice-stuffed peppers

 Stuffed vegetables are always a popular dish. Brown rice is an excellent source of magnesium, fiber, and some of the B vitamins.

ingredients

- 4 large bell peppers
- 1 tbsp olive oil
- 4 shallots, finely chopped
- 1 clove garlic, crushed
- 1½ cups/4 ounces (115g) finely chopped mushrooms
- 1 zucchini, finely chopped
- 1¼ cups/6 ounces (175g) cooked brown rice
- 2 tomatoes, peeled, seeded, and finely chopped
- ⅓ cup/2 ounces (55g) finely chopped pine nuts
- ½ cup finely chopped, pitted black olives
- 2 tbsp chopped fresh mixed herbs
- sea salt
- freshly ground black pepper

serves *four*
preparation time *25 minutes*
cooking time *35–40 minutes*

method

1 Preheat the oven to 350°F.
2 Slice the tops off the peppers; remove and discard the cores and seeds. Blanch in boiling water for 4 minutes, then drain.
3 Heat the oil in a pan. Add the shallots, garlic, mushrooms, and zucchini and cook for 5 minutes, stirring occasionally. Remove from the heat, and add all the remaining ingredients.
4 Spoon some stuffing into each pepper and top with the lids. Place in a shallow ovenproof dish and add a little water. Cover with foil and bake for 35–40 minutes, until tender.
5 Serve with a dark leaf salad.

variations

- *Use almonds or hazelnuts instead of pine nuts.*
- *Use 1 leek instead of the shallots.*
- *Use couscous instead of rice.*

starch-based *meals*

potato, leek, *and* cilantro rösti

 This appetizing way of serving potatoes is sure to be popular. Potatoes are rich in dietary fiber, potassium, and vitamin C.

■ ingredients

- 1½ pounds (700g) potatoes, washed and left whole and unpeeled
- 2tbsp olive oil
- 2 leeks, washed and thinly sliced
- 2–3tbsp chopped fresh cilantro
- sea salt
- freshly ground black pepper

serves *four to six*
preparation time *15 minutes, plus cooling time*
cooking time *20–25 minutes*

■ method

1 Preheat the oven to 425°F.

2 Grease two baking trays.

3 Parboil the potatoes in a pan of boiling water for 6 minutes. Drain and set aside to cool slightly.

4 When cool enough to handle, peel the potatoes and coarsely grate them into a bowl. Set aside.

5 Heat the oil in a large nonstick skillet. Add the leeks and cook for about 5 minutes, until softened, stirring occasionally. Remove the skillet from the heat.

6 Add the leeks, cilantro, and seasoning to the potatoes and stir. Spoon 12 small mounds of the potato mixture onto the prepared baking trays.

7 Bake for 20–25 minutes until golden brown and crisp.

8 Serve immediately, with cooked fresh vegetables, such as spinach and broiled tomatoes.

variations

• *Use 2 onions instead of the leeks.*

• *Use chopped fresh parsley, basil, or tarragon instead of cilantro.*

tomato *and* pea couscous salad

Couscous is a good grain base for a salad. Tossed with vegetables and a light, flavorsome dressing, it makes a tasty lunch dish. Tomatoes and peppers are rich sources of vitamin C; tomatoes also provide lycopene, a potential anti-cancer compound.

ingredients

- 1½ cups/8 ounces (225g) quick-cook couscous
- 1¼ cups/8 ounces (225g) fresh or frozen peas
- 12 ounces (350g) cherry tomatoes, halved
- 1 yellow bell pepper, seeded and diced
- 6–8 green onions, chopped
- half an English cucumber, diced

for the dressing

- ⅔ cup/¼ pint (150ml) tomato juice
- 1 clove garlic, crushed
- 2tsp balsamic vinegar
- ½tsp brown sugar
- 2tbsp chopped fresh cilantro
- sea salt
- freshly ground black pepper

serves *four to six*
preparation time *15 minutes, plus cooling and standing time*
cooking time *10–15 minutes*

method

1 Soak and cook the couscous according to packet directions. Set aside to cool; then place in a large serving bowl.

2 Cook the peas in a pan of boiling water for 3–5 minutes, until cooked and tender. Drain well, then rinse under cold running water to cool quickly, and drain again.

3 Stir the peas, tomatoes, yellow bell pepper, green onions, and cucumber into the couscous.

4 Place all the remaining ingredients in a small bowl and whisk together. Pour over the couscous salad and toss the ingredients together.

5 Cover and leave at room temperature for 1 hour before serving, or cover and chill for several hours before serving, to let the flavors blend.

6 Serve with a mixed dark leaf salad.

variations

• *Use pasta instead of couscous. Cook in a large pan of lightly salted, boiling water for about 8–10 minutes (or cook according to the packet directions).*

• *Use regular or plum tomatoes instead of cherry tomatoes.*

roasted vegetables *with* garlic *and* fresh herbs

This is a simple but delicious way of serving mixed vegetables. The addition of artichokes adds flavor and texture as well as plentiful supplies of beta carotene, folic acid, and most minerals.

ingredients

2 onions, each cut into 8 pieces

4 zucchini, cut into chunks

1 red bell pepper, seeded and cut into large chunks

1 yellow bell pepper, seeded and cut into large chunks

8 ounces (225g) button mushrooms

6 ounces (175g) baby corn

2 cloves garlic, finely chopped

2tbsp olive oil

4 tomatoes, halved

1 14-ounce (400g) can artichoke hearts, rinsed, drained, and halved

2–3tbsp chopped fresh mixed herbs

sea salt

freshly ground black pepper

serves *four to six*
preparation time *15 minutes*
cooking time *30–35 minutes*

method

1 Preheat the oven to 425°F.
2 Put the onions, zucchini, peppers, mushrooms, corn, and garlic in a large roasting pan and stir to mix. Add the oil and toss the vegetables in the oil, coating them lightly all over.
3 Bake for 20 minutes, stirring once.
4 Add the tomatoes and artichoke hearts and stir. Bake for another 10–15 minutes, until the vegetables are just cooked and are tinged brown at the edges.
5 Sprinkle with the herbs and seasoning over the vegetables. Stir and serve hot with a mixed dark leaf salad.

variations

• *Use a mixture of baby vegetables.*
• *Use 9 ounces (250g) cherry tomatoes instead of regular ones.*
• *Use sesame oil instead of olive oil.*

vegetable-based

carrot, zucchini, *and* broccoli stir-fry

 This stir-fry of vegetables makes a great light meal or snack. Carrots and broccoli are excellent sources of carotenoids.

ingredients

- 2tbsp olive oil

- 2 carrots, cut into matchstick (julienne) strips

- 2 zucchini, cut into matchstick (julienne) strips

- 8 ounces (225g) small broccoli florets, halved

- 1 large clove garlic, finely chopped

- 1-inch (2.5cm) piece of fresh ginger root, peeled and finely chopped or grated

- 4 ounces (115g) bean sprouts

- 1 tbsp fresh lemon juice

- 1 tbsp light soy sauce

- sea salt

- freshly ground black pepper

serves *four*
preparation time *15 minutes*
cooking time *5–7 minutes*

method

1 Heat the oil in a nonstick wok or large skillet. Add the carrots, zucchini, broccoli, garlic, and ginger, and stir-fry over a high heat for 4–5 minutes.

2 Add the bean sprouts, lemon juice, and soy sauce, and stir-fry for another 1–2 minutes, until the vegetables are just cooked.

3 Season to taste with salt and pepper and serve hot with broiled tomatoes and bell peppers.

variations

- *Use cauliflower florets or sliced cremini mushrooms instead of broccoli florets.*
- *Use 2 cups/4 ounces (115g) shredded spinach instead of zucchini.*
- *Use dry sherry instead of lemons.*
- *Use sesame oil instead of olive oil.*

vegetable-based

oven-baked vegetable compote

 This vegetable compote provides a range of nutrients, including beta carotene (for vitamin A), vitamin C, selenium, and iron.

ingredients

- 1 14-ounce (400g) can chopped tomatoes
- 2tsp dried *herbes de provence*
- sea salt
- freshly ground black pepper
- 1 onion, thinly sliced
- 2 leeks, washed and thinly sliced
- 4 celery stalks chopped
- 1 red bell pepper, seeded and sliced
- 1 yellow bell pepper, seeded and sliced
- 1 small eggplant, thickly sliced
- 2 zucchini, sliced
- 2 carrots, thinly sliced
- 4 ounces (115g) button mushrooms
- fresh herb sprigs, to garnish

serves *four to six*
preparation time *15 minutes*
cooking time *1 hour*

method

1 Preheat the oven to 375°F.
2 Put the tomatoes, dried herbs, and seasoning in a large ovenproof casserole and stir. Add all the remaining ingredients.
3 Cover and bake for about 1 hour, until the vegetables are cooked and tender, stirring once or twice.
4 Garnish with the herb sprigs and serve hot, either on its own or with a chopped mixed salad.

variations
- *Use 6 shallots instead of onion.*
- *Use 1¼ cups/6 ounces (175g) diced rutabaga or turnip instead of carrots.*
- *Use baby corn instead of button mushrooms.*

freezing instructions
Let cool completely, then transfer to a rigid, freezeproof container. Cover, seal, and label. Freeze for up to 3 months. Defrost and reheat gently in a medium oven.

vegetable-based

vegetable curry

 This mild vegetable curry makes a filling evening meal. Vegetables contain many nutrients, including beta carotene (for vitamin A), vitamin C, potassium, and fiber. Extra virgin olive oil is a monounsaturated fat.

ingredients

- 1tbsp olive oil
- 1 large onion, sliced
- 2 cloves garlic, finely chopped
- 1 small fresh red chili, finely chopped
- 2¼ pounds (1 kg) mixed prepared fresh vegetables, including diced potatoes, rutabaga, turnip, carrots, and parsnips, with small cauliflower florets and peas left whole
- 2tsp ground coriander
- 2tsp ground cumin
- 1½tsp ground turmeric
- 1 14-ounce (400g) can chopped tomatoes
- ⅔ cup/¼ pint (150ml) vegetable stock (see recipe on page 20)
- ⅔ cup/¼ pint (150ml) coconut milk
- sea salt
- freshly ground black pepper
- 1tbsp cornstarch
- 2tbsp chopped fresh cilantro, to garnish

serves *four to six*
preparation time *15 minutes*
cooking time *35–50 minutes*

method

1 Heat the oil in a pan. Add the onion, garlic, and chili and cook for 5 minutes.
2 Stir in all the remaining ingredients except the fresh cilantro garnish. Cover and bring to a boil; then reduce the heat and simmer for 30–45 minutes, until the vegetables are cooked and tender, stirring occasionally.
3 Blend the cornstarch with 4tbsp water and stir into the curry. Bring to a boil, stirring continuously, then simmer for 2 minutes.
4 Serve the curry on a bed of couscous or brown rice. Garnish with the chopped cilantro.

variations

- Use 3–4tsp curry powder instead of the fresh chili and ground spices.
- Use 8 shallots instead of the onion.
- Use additional stock instead of coconut milk.
- If you prefer a hot curry, add more ground spices to suit your own taste.

freezing instructions

Let cool completely, then transfer to a rigid, freezeproof container. Cover, seal, and label. Freeze for up to 3 months. Defrost and reheat gently in a pan.

vegetable-based

skin *and* nail foods

FOR HEALTHY SKIN *and nails, the body needs sufficient amounts of all the vitamins, as well as calcium, iron, selenium, and zinc. The vitamin B group is important for the repair and regeneration of skin tissue—signs of deficiency include cracks and sores around the mouth and nose.*

Vitamin C is used in the production of collagen, which is vital for wound healing and protecting against infection. Common signs of vitamin C deficiency are bleeding gums, cuts that won't heal, and broken capillaries. Pale, concave nails and itchy skin may indicate iron deficiency.

watercress soup

 This warming soup is good served with whole-wheat bread. Watercress is a great skin food, rich in carotenoids and vitamin C.

■ ingredients

- 1 tbsp olive oil
- 1 onion, chopped
- 1½ cups/8 ounces (225g) diced potatoes
- 3 celery stalks, finely chopped
- 2 cups/8 ounces (225g) roughly chopped watercress
- 2½ cups/1 pint (600ml) vegetable stock (see recipe on page 20)
- 1¼ cups/½ pint (300ml) milk
- sea salt
- freshly ground black pepper
- small watercress sprigs, to garnish

serves *four*
preparation time *15 minutes*
cooking time *20–25 minutes*

■ method

1 Heat the oil in a large pan. Add the onion, potatoes, and celery. Cook gently for 5 minutes, stirring occasionally.
2 Add the chopped watercress, stock, milk, and seasoning, and mix well. Cover and bring to a boil; then reduce the heat and simmer for 15–20 minutes, stirring occasionally, until the vegetables are cooked and tender.
3 Remove the pan from the heat. Cool the soup slightly, then purée in a blender or food processor until smooth.

4 Return the soup to the rinsed-out pan and reheat gently until hot, stirring occasionally.
5 To serve, ladle into warmed soup bowls and garnish with small watercress sprigs.
6 Serve with whole-wheat bread or rolls.

variations

- *For a delicious broccoli soup, replace the watercress with 12 ounces (350g) broccoli florets.*
- *Use sweet potatoes instead of standard potatoes.*
- *Use 6 shallots or 1 leek instead of the onion.*

soups *and* appetizers

shredded beet *and* carrot salad

This salad of shredded root vegetables and dark salad leaves is tossed in a honey-lemon dressing. Beets are an excellent source of folate, vitamin C, magnesium, and potassium.

ingredients

- 12 ounces (350g) carrots
- 8 ounces (225g) raw beets
- 4 ounces (115g) mixed dark salad leaves, such as spinach, watercress, lollo rosso (coral lettuce), and red (ruby) chard
- 2tbsp chopped fresh mixed herbs
- $^1/_4$–$^1/_2$ cup/1–2 ounces (25–55g) roughly chopped toasted hazelnuts

for the dressing

- 2tbsp hazelnut oil
- 1tbsp olive oil
- juice of 1 lemon
- 1tbsp honey
- 1 clove garlic, crushed
- sea salt
- freshly ground black pepper

serves *four*
preparation time *15 minutes*

method

1 Peel and coarsely grate or shred the carrots and beets. Put in a bowl.
2 Add the salad leaves and mixed herbs, and toss. Divide the salad between four serving plates.
3 Put the oils, lemon juice, honey, garlic, and seasoning in a bowl, and whisk until thoroughly mixed.
4 Drizzle the dressing over the salads and toss.
5 Scatter some hazelnuts over each salad.
6 Serve immediately with thick slices of whole-wheat bread.

variations

• Use *lime juice instead of lemon.*
• Use *zucchini instead of beets.*
• Use *almonds or pecans instead of hazelnuts.*

soups *and* appetizers

broiled mackerel *with* cucumber relish

In this quick and easy recipe, fresh mackerel are accompanied by a tasty cucumber relish. Oily fish such as mackerel are a good source of vitamins A and D, B vitamins, selenium, and omega-3 essential fatty acids, all of which are good skin and nail nutrients.

ingredients

- 2 pounds (900g) small mackerel, gutted and cleaned, if wished
- 2tbsp olive oil
- juice of 1 lime
- 1tsp dried mixed herbs

for the relish

- half an English cucumber, finely chopped
- 2 shallots, finely chopped
- 1 clove garlic, crushed
- ⅔ cup/5½ ounces (150g) plain yogurt
- 1–2tbsp chopped fresh mint
- sea salt
- freshly ground black pepper

serves *four to six*
preparation time *15 minutes*
cooking time *8–14 minutes*

method

1 Put the cucumber, shallots, garlic, yogurt, mint, and seasoning in a bowl, and mix well. Cover and set aside.

2 Preheat the broiler to high. Cover a broiler rack with foil and place the mackerel on the prepared broiler rack.

3 Put the oil, lime juice, dried herbs, and seasoning in a bowl and mix thoroughly. Brush the mackerel lightly all over with the oil mixture.

4 Broil the mackerel for about 4–7 minutes on each side, until they are cooked.

5 Place the mackerel on serving dishes with the cucumber relish alongside.

6 Serve with baked potatoes and a crisp green salad.

variations

• Use other small oily fish instead of mackerel.

• Use fresh basil instead of mint.

• Use lemon or orange juice instead of lime juice.

• Use 4 chopped green onions instead of shallots.

fish *dishes*

chinese roast lemon chicken

Serve this delicious lemon chicken with crisp roasted potatoes and fresh vegetables for an appetizing meal. Poultry is a good source of protein and B vitamins, nutrients for skin and hair health.

ingredients

- 1 tbsp light soy sauce
- 1 tbsp dry sherry
- rind and juice of 1 lemon
- 2 shallots, chopped
- 2-inch (5cm) piece fresh ginger root, peeled and chopped
- 2 tbsp chopped fresh cilantro
- sea salt
- freshly ground black pepper
- 1¾-pound (1.5 kg) whole chicken
- 1 whole lemon, thickly sliced
- 2 tbsp/1 ounce (25g) melted butter
- 1¼ cups/½ pint (300ml) chicken stock (see recipe on page 20)

serves *four*
preparation time *15 minutes*
cooking time *1½ hours*

method

1 Preheat the oven to 400°F.

2 Put the soy sauce, sherry, lemon rind and juice, shallots, ginger root, cilantro, and seasoning in a blender or food processor and blend until fairly smooth and well mixed.

3 Lift the skin flap on the chicken and loosen the skin over the breast, trying to avoid breaking the skin. Insert the puréed mixture under the skin and spread it out in an even layer.

4 Put the lemon slices in the cavity of the chicken.

5 Weigh the bird and calculate the cooking time, allowing 20 minutes per 1 pound (450g), plus 20 minutes.

6 Place the chicken in a roasting pan and brush all over with the melted butter. Pour the stock around the base of the chicken.

7 Roast, uncovered, for about 1½ hours, until the chicken is cooked and tender and the juices run clear. Cover the chicken with foil once it is well browned.

8 Carve the chicken and serve with roasted potatoes, braised carrots, and celery.

variations

• *For poached lemon chicken, follow the recipe above, but do not brush the chicken with butter. Put the chicken in a large pan and cover with water. Cover, bring to a boil, and poach gently for 50–60 minutes, until the chicken is cooked and tender. Carve into slices and serve. The poaching liquid can be boiled rapidly until reduced to make a tasty sauce to accompany the chicken.*

• *Use lime instead of lemon.*

• *Use chopped fresh tarragon instead of cilantro.*

meat and poultry dishes

turkey *and* brussels sprouts stir-fry

 Using sunflower seeds adds flavor and texture to this quick and easy stir-fry. Sunflower seeds are an especially good source of vitamin E.

ingredients

- 1 tbsp sesame oil
- 12 ounces (350g) skinless, boneless turkey cutlets, cut into thin strips
- 1 clove garlic, crushed
- 3 cups/8 ounces (225g) shredded Brussels sprouts
- 1 red bell pepper, seeded and sliced
- 6–8 green onions, chopped
- 6 ounces (175g) cremini mushrooms, sliced
- 2 tbsp dry sherry
- 2 tbsp light soy sauce
- freshly ground black pepper
- 1–2 tbsp sunflower seeds

serves *four*
preparation time *15 minutes*
cooking time *8–10 minutes*

method

1 Heat the oil in a nonstick wok or large skillet. Add the turkey and garlic and stir-fry over a high heat for 2 minutes.

2 Add the sprouts and red pepper and stir-fry for 2–3 minutes.

3 Add the green onions and mushrooms and stir-fry for another 2–3 minutes.

4 Add the sherry, soy sauce, and black pepper and stir-fry until the mixture is piping hot and the turkey and vegetables are cooked and tender.

5 Scatter the sunflower seeds over the turkey.

6 Serve with brown rice or rice noodles.

variations

• *Use chicken breast or lean lamb instead of turkey.*
• *Use zucchini or carrots instead of Brussels sprouts.*
• *Use unsweetened apple juice instead of sherry.*

meat *and* poultry *dishes*

roasted sweet potatoes

Roasted sweet potatoes make a great accompaniment to roast lean meat or fish. Red-fleshed sweet potatoes are rich in beta carotene (which the body can convert to vitamin A), potassium, and vitamin C, all excellent skin and nail foods.

ingredients

- 2¼ pounds (1 kg) red-fleshed sweet potatoes
- 2–3tbsp olive oil
- 1 large clove garlic, finely chopped
- 1–2tbsp chopped fresh rosemary
- sea salt
- freshly ground black pepper

serves *four*
preparation time *15 minutes*
cooking time *45 minutes*

method

1 Preheat the oven to 425°F.
2 Peel the potatoes. Cut them into chunks and put into a pan with cold, lightly salted water. Cover with a lid, bring to a boil, and boil for 2 minutes. Drain well.
3 Heat the oil in a roasting pan in the oven for 3–4 minutes.
4 Add the potatoes, garlic, rosemary, and seasoning and turn the potatoes over in the oil mixture, coating them completely.
5 Roast the potatoes for about 45 minutes, until golden brown and crisp, turning once or twice. Drain off any excess oil after about 35 minutes.
6 Serve with meat or grilled fish, and cooked vegetables, such as broccoli and cauliflower florets.

variations

- *Use parsnips or celeriac instead of sweet potatoes.*
- *Use fresh thyme or cilantro instead of rosemary.*

vegetable *dishes*

fruit *and* nut rice salad

This delicious rice salad is excellent for a summertime picnic or buffet meal. Nuts such as Brazils and almonds are great skin foods because they contain potassium, magnesium, selenium, iron, and zinc.

ingredients

- 1¼ cups/8 ounces (225g) brown rice
- 1 yellow bell pepper, seeded and diced
- 6–8 green onions, chopped
- 2 red-skinned eating apples
- 1½ cups/6 ounces (175g) chopped dried apricots
- ⅔ cup/4 ounces (115g) golden raisins
- ⅔ cup/4 ounces (115g) raisins
- ¾ cup/3 ounces (85g) roughly chopped Brazil nuts
- ¾ cup/3 ounces (85g) roughly chopped almonds

for the dressing

- ⅔ cup/¼ pint (150ml) unsweetened orange juice
- 2tbsp olive oil
- 1tbsp whole-grain mustard
- 1tbsp balsamic vinegar
- 2tbsp chopped fresh parsley
- sea salt and ground black pepper

serves *six*
preparation time *15 minutes*
cooking time *30 minutes*

method

1 Cook the rice until tender. Rinse under cold running water and drain.
2 Put the cold rice in a serving bowl. Add the pepper, green onions, apples, apricots, golden raisins, raisins, and nuts, and mix.
3 Put all the dressing ingredients in a bowl and whisk together.
4 Pour the dressing over the rice salad and toss the ingredients.
5 Serve with broiled lean meat or baked fish.

variations

- *Use dried pears, peaches, or figs instead of apricots.*
- *Use unsweetened apple or grape juice instead of orange juice.*
- *Use mixed brown and wild rice.*
- *Add a few raw pumpkin seeds for their essential fatty acids and iron.*

vegetable *dishes*

poached pears *with* blackcurrant sauce

 Fresh pears poached with whole spices and served with a blackcurrant sauce make a delicious dessert. Blackcurrants contain various antioxidants, including large amounts of vitamin C.

ingredients

- 1¼ cups/½ pint (300ml) unsweetened apple juice or grape juice
- ⅓ cup/3 ounces (85g) dark brown sugar
- 6 ripe pears, peeled and left whole with stalks intact
- pared rind of 1 lemon
- 1 cinnamon stick, broken in half
- 6 whole cloves
- 1½ cups/8 ounces (225g) fresh or frozen blackcurrants, defrosted
- 2tsp arrowroot
- 2tbsp crème de cassis or blackcurrant liqueur
- fresh mint sprigs, to decorate

serves *six*
preparation time *10 minutes*
cooking time *40 minutes*

method

1 Put the apple or grape juice and sugar in a pan and heat gently until the sugar has dissolved, stirring continuously.

2 Add the pears, lemon rind, cinnamon stick, and cloves and stir. Cover and bring to a boil; then reduce the heat and simmer for about 15 minutes, until the pears are cooked and tender.

3 Using a slotted spoon, remove the pears and put them in a serving dish. Cover and keep them warm.

4 Remove and discard the lemon rind, cinnamon stick, and cloves.

5 Add the blackcurrants to the pan. Cover and bring to a boil; then reduce the heat and simmer for about 10 minutes, until soft, stirring occasionally.

6 Blend the arrowroot with the crème de cassis or liqueur and stir into the blackcurrant sauce. Heat gently, stirring continuously, until the sauce comes to a boil and thickens slightly.

7 Pour the blackcurrant sauce over the pears and decorate with fresh mint sprigs.

8 Serve warm or cold with plain yogurt or homemade yogurt ice.

variations

- *Use firm, ripe peaches or nectarines instead of pears.*
- *Use raspberries or blueberries instead of blackcurrants.*
- *Add an extra teaspoon of arrowroot if you prefer a thicker sauce.*
- *Sprinkle with raw wheat germ or brewer's yeast for vitamin B.*

desserts   bakes

broiled nectarines *with* honey *and* spices

This simple dessert is quick to make and delicious to eat. Serve it with yogurt, crème fraîche, or light sour cream. Nectarines and peaches are good for skin health as they contain plenty of vitamin C.

■ ingredients

- 4 large ripe nectarines
- 2tbsp unsweetened orange juice
- 2tbsp honey
- 1–2tsp ground cinnamon

serves *two to four*
preparation time *10 minutes*
cooking time *4–5 minutes*

■ method

1 Put the nectarines in a large pan of boiling water for 15 seconds. Remove using a slotted spoon and plunge them into a bowl of cold water. Drain, then peel off the skins using a sharp knife.
2 Preheat the broiler to high. Cover a broiler rack with foil. Cut each nectarine in half and remove the pit, then cut the fruit into quarters or slices. Place the nectarines on the broiler rack.
3 Put the orange juice, honey, and spice in a bowl and stir. Drizzle the mixture over the nectarines.
4 Broil the nectarines for about 4–5 minutes, until hot, turning once or twice. Serve hot with plain yogurt, crème fraîche. or light sour cream.

variations

- Use peaches instead of nectarines.
- Use ground ginger instead of cinnamon.
- Use maple syrup instead of honey.

desserts *and* bakes

banana *and* date loaf

Serve this delicately spiced banana and tea loaf in slices on its own, or spread with a little butter or honey. Bananas contain a number of skin- and nail-boosting nutrients.

ingredients

- 2 cups/8 ounces (225g) whole-wheat flour
- 2tsp baking powder
- 1tsp ground nutmeg
- ½ cup/4 ounces (115g) butter
- ½ cup/4 ounces (115g) light brown sugar
- ⅓ cup/4 ounces (115g) thick honey
- 2 medium-sized eggs, beaten
- 2 large bananas, peeled and mashed with a little lemon juice
- ⅔ cup/4 ounces (115g) finely chopped dried dates

serves *eight to ten*
preparation time *20 minutes*
cooking time *1–1¼ hours*

method

1 Preheat the oven to 350°F. Grease and line a 2-pound loaf pan.
2 Put the flour, baking powder, and nutmeg in a bowl. Lightly rub in the butter until the mixture resembles bread crumbs.
3 Add the sugar, honey, eggs, bananas, and dates and beat well until thoroughly mixed. Turn the mixture into the prepared loaf pan.
4 Bake for 1–1¼ hours, until well-risen and firm to the touch.
5 Cool slightly in the pan, then turn out onto a wire rack to cool.
6 Serve in slices on its own or spread with a little butter, preserve, or honey.

variations

* Brush the top of the cooked, cold loaf with warmed honey and sprinkle with demerara sugar before serving.
* Use maple syrup instead of honey.
* Add the finely grated rind of 1 lemon or 1 small orange to the mixture before baking.
* Use chopped walnuts or dried apricots instead of dates.

freezing instructions

Let cool completely, then wrap in foil or seal in a freezer bag and label. Freeze for up to 3 months. Defrost thoroughly for several hours at room temperature before serving.

desserts bakes

peaches *and* cream

FEED YOUR FACE *with this skin- and nail-boosting menu from the skin and nail foods section. Vitamin and mineral deficiencies will* manifest as pallid, dull skin and brittle nails, so eat the right foods to help ensure that healthier nails and a more glowing complexion will be yours!*

shredded beet *and* carrot salad

Beets contain numerous vitamins and minerals to help improve the condition of your skin.

■ ingredients

- 12 ounces (350g) carrots
- 8 ounces (225g) raw beets
- 4 ounces (115g) mixed dark salad leaves such as spinach, watercress, lollo rosso (coral lettuce), and red (ruby) chard
- 2tbsp chopped fresh mixed herbs
- ¼–½ cup/1–2 ounces (25–55g) roughly chopped toasted hazelnuts

for the dressing

- 2tbsp hazelnut oil
- 1tbsp olive oil
- juice of 1 lemon
- 1tbsp honey
- 1 clove garlic, crushed
- sea salt
- freshly ground black pepper

serves *four*
preparation time *15 minutes*

■ method

1 Peel and coarsely grate or shred the carrots and beets. Put in a bowl.
2 Add the salad leaves and mixed herbs, and toss. Divide the salad between four serving plates.
3 Put the oils, lemon juice, honey, garlic, and seasoning in a bowl, and whisk until thoroughly mixed.
4 Drizzle the dressing over the salads and toss.
5 Scatter some hazelnuts over each salad.
6 Serve immediately with thick slices of whole-wheat bread.

turkey *and* brussels sprouts stir-fry

The protein and B vitamins in turkey make this delicious main course a skin helper.

■ ingredients

- 1tbsp sesame oil
- 12 ounces (350g) skinless, boneless turkey cutlets, cut into thin strips
- 1 clove garlic, crushed
- 3 cups/8 ounces (225g) shredded Brussels sprouts
- 1 red bell pepper, seeded and sliced
- 6–8 green onions, chopped
- 6 ounces (175g) cremini mushrooms, sliced
- 2tbsp dry sherry

- 2tbsp light soy sauce
- freshly ground black pepper
- 1–2tbsp sunflower seeds

serves *four*
preparation time *15 minutes*
cooking time *8–10 minutes*

method

1 Heat the oil in a nonstick wok or large skillet. Add the turkey and garlic and stir-fry over a high heat for 2 minutes.
2 Add the sprouts and red pepper and stir-fry for 2–3 minutes.
3 Add the green onions and mushrooms and stir-fry for another 2–3 minutes.
4 Add the sherry, soy sauce, and black pepper and stir-fry until the mixture is piping hot and the turkey and vegetables are cooked and tender.
5 Scatter the sunflower seeds over the turkey.
6 Serve with brown rice or rice noodles.

poached pears *with* blackcurrant sauce

The vitamin C in blackcurrants (important for healthy skin and manufacture of collagen) rounds off this nutritious skincare menu.

ingredients

- 1¼ cups/½ pint (300ml) unsweetened apple juice or grape juice
- ⅓ cup/3 ounces (85g) dark brown sugar
- 6 ripe pears, peeled and left whole with stalks intact
- pared rind of 1 lemon
- 1 cinnamon stick, broken in half
- 6 whole cloves
- 1½ cups/8 ounces (225g) fresh or frozen blackcurrants, defrosted
- 2tsp arrowroot
- 2tbsp crème de cassis or blackcurrant liqueur
- fresh mint sprigs, to decorate

serves *six*
preparation time *10 minutes*
cooking time *40 minutes*

method

1 Put the apple or grape juice and sugar in a pan and heat gently until the sugar has dissolved, stirring continuously.
2 Add the pears, lemon rind, cinnamon stick, and cloves and stir. Cover and bring to a boil; then reduce the heat and simmer for about 15 minutes, until the pears are cooked and tender.
3 Using a slotted spoon, remove the pears and put them in a serving dish. Cover and keep them warm.
4 Remove and discard the lemon rind, cinnamon stick, and cloves.
5 Add the blackcurrants to the pan. Cover and bring to a boil; then reduce the heat and simmer for about 10 minutes, until soft, stirring occasionally.
6 Blend the arrowroot with the crème de cassis or liqueur and stir into the blackcurrant sauce. Heat gently, stirring continuously, until the sauce comes to a boil and thickens slightly.
7 Pour the blackcurrant sauce over the pears and decorate with fresh mint sprigs.
8 Serve warm or cold with plain yogurt or homemade yogurt ice.

hair *foods*

THE CONDITION OF *your hair is a clear indication of your general health and well-being. People suffering from physical stress may be short of B vitamins, which are essential for healthy hair. A deficiency of vitamin A may cause dry* hair, *so you should ensure that your diet includes plenty of carrots, dark-green leafy vegetables, sweet potatoes, and apricots. Abnormal hair loss and a dry scalp may signal a severe zinc deficiency—foods that are rich in zinc include seafood, poultry, eggs, grains, and legumes.*

spicy carrot *and* barley soup

This hot, spicy soup, served with crusty whole-wheat bread or rolls, is great for chilly winter days. Carrots provide beta carotene, which the body converts into vitamin A, an important nutrient for healthy hair.

ingredients

- 1tbsp olive oil
- 1 onion, finely chopped
- 3 cups/1 pound (450g) finely chopped carrots
- 2 celery stalks, finely chopped
- ¼ cup/2 ounces (55g) pearl barley
- 2tsp ground cumin
- 2tsp ground coriander
- 1tsp hot chili powder (optional)
- 3½ cups/1½ pints (850ml) vegetable stock (see recipe on page 20)
- sea salt and ground black pepper
- fresh flat-leaf parsley, to garnish

serves *four*
preparation time *10 minutes*
cooking time *1¼ hours*

method

1 Heat the oil in a large pan. Add the onion and cook for 5 minutes, stirring occasionally.
2 Add the carrots, celery, pearl barley, and ground spices. Cook for 1 minute, stirring continuously. Stir in the stock.
3 Cover and bring to a boil; then reduce the heat and simmer for about 1¼ hours, stirring occasionally, until the barley is cooked and tender. Season to taste with salt and pepper.
4 Ladle into warmed soup bowls and garnish with chopped fresh flatleaf parsley.
5 Serve with whole-wheat bread.

variations

- *Omit the barley, if preferred. Cook the soup as directed for about 45 minutes, then purée in a blender or food processor until smooth. Reheat before serving.*
- *Use 1 large leek instead of the onion.*
- *Use parsnips or rutabaga instead of carrots.*

freezing instructions

Let cool completely, then transfer to a rigid, freezeproof container. Cover, seal, and label. Freeze for up to 3 months. Defrost and reheat gently in a pan until piping hot.

soups *and* appetizers

melon *and* shrimp appetizer

Melons filled with shrimp tossed in a light dressing make a popular appetizer. Orange-fleshed melons are the most nutritious of the many varieties of melon. They are a rich source of beta carotene, a vitamin A precursor.

ingredients

- 2 small orange-fleshed melons
- 4tbsp mayonnaise (see recipe on page 21)
- 2tbsp plain yogurt
- 2tbsp chopped fresh parsley
- 1tsp finely grated lemon rind
- sea salt
- freshly ground black pepper
- 12 ounces (350g) cooked, shelled shrimp
- fresh parsley sprigs, to garnish

serves *four*
preparation time *15 minutes*

method

1 Halve the melons and remove and discard the seeds. Place each half on a serving plate.
2 Put the mayonnaise, yogurt, chopped parsley, lemon rind, and seasoning in a bowl. Fold in the shrimp and mix well.
3 Pile the shrimp mixture into the melon halves and garnish with fresh parsley sprigs.
4 Serve with fingers of lightly buttered whole-wheat bread.

variations

• *Use fresh, flaked crab or canned tuna or salmon, instead of shrimp.*
• *Use avocados instead of melons.*
• *Use chopped fresh cilantro instead of parsley.*
• *Use grated lime rind instead of lemon rind.*

spinach *and* avocado salad

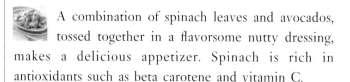

A combination of spinach leaves and avocados, tossed together in a flavorsome nutty dressing, makes a delicious appetizer. Spinach is rich in antioxidants such as beta carotene and vitamin C.

ingredients

- 6 ounces (175g) baby spinach leaves
- half an English cucumber, sliced
- 4 celery stalks, chopped
- 2 large ripe avocados
- juice of 1 lemon

for the dressing
- 4tbsp hazelnut or olive oil
- 2–3tsp balsamic vinegar
- 1 clove garlic, crushed
- 1tsp honey
- 1tbsp chopped fresh parsley
- 1tbsp chopped fresh chives
- sea salt
- freshly ground black pepper

serves *six*
preparation time *15 minutes*

method

1 Put the spinach leaves, cucumber, and celery in a bowl.
2 Peel, pit, and slice or chop the avocados. Toss them in the lemon juice, add to the salad, and stir gently.
3 To make the dressing, put all the dressing ingredients in a bowl and whisk together. Drizzle over the salad and toss well.
4 Serve immediately, with thick slices of whole-wheat bread.

variations

• *Use 2 zucchini instead of the cucumber.*
• *Use 1 small green bell pepper, seeded and diced, instead of celery.*
• *Use 1 medium orange-fleshed melon instead of the avocados.*

tagliatelle *with* salmon, zucchini, *and* almonds

This freshly cooked pasta with a tasty salmon and zucchini sauce, topped with toasted almonds, will be a popular choice. Almonds are a good source of vitamins E and B$_2$ and minerals such as magnesium and phosphorus.

ingredients

- 2tbsp/1 ounce (25g) butter
- 8 ounces (225g) leeks, washed and thinly sliced
- 8 ounces (225g) zucchini, thinly sliced
- ¼ cup/1 ounce (25g) whole-wheat flour
- 1¾ cups/¾ pint (425ml) vegetable stock (see recipe on page 20)
- ⅔ cup/¼ pint (150ml) dry white wine
- 1 14-ounce (400g) can salmon in water, drained and flaked
- 1–2tbsp chopped fresh tarragon
- dash of Tabasco sauce
- sea salt
- freshly ground black pepper
- 12 ounces (350g) tagliatelle
- ½ cup/2 ounces (55g) toasted flaked almonds
- fresh tarragon sprigs, to garnish

serves *four*
preparation time *10 minutes*
cooking time *20 minutes*

method

1 Melt the butter in a pan and add the leeks and zucchini. Cover and cook gently for about 10 minutes, until softened, stirring occasionally.
2 Add the flour and cook gently for 1 minute, stirring. Gradually stir in the stock and wine, then bring slowly to a boil, stirring continuously, until the sauce thickens. Simmer gently for 2 minutes, stirring.
3 Stir the salmon, chopped tarragon, Tabasco sauce, and seasoning into the sauce. Reheat gently until piping hot, stirring.
4 Cook the tagliatelle in a large pan of lightly salted, boiling water according to the directions on the package.
5 Drain the pasta thoroughly and transfer to warmed serving plates. Spoon the salmon sauce over the pasta and scatter with almonds. Garnish with fresh tarragon sprigs.
6 Serve hot with a mixed dark leaf salad.

variations

- *Use 1 onion instead of leeks.*
- *Use canned tuna instead of salmon.*
- *Use fresh flat-leaf parsley or cilantro instead of tarragon.*

fish *dishes*

baked trout *with* lemon *and* almonds

Trout baked with lemon juice and almonds makes a tasty and nutritious dish. Oily fish such as trout provide vitamins A and D, and omega-3 fatty acids, all of which are good hair nutrients.

ingredients

- 4 rainbow trout, each weighing about 10 ounces (280g), gutted and cleaned, with the heads and tails left on
- finely grated rind and juice of 2 lemons
- 3tbsp/1½ ounces (40g) melted butter
- 3tbsp chopped fresh parsley
- sea salt
- freshly ground black pepper
- ½ cup/2 ounces (55g) flaked almonds

serves *four*
preparation time *10 minutes*
cooking time *20–25 minutes*

method

1 Preheat the oven to 350°F.
2 Place the trout side-by-side in a shallow, ovenproof dish. Make three diagonal slashes on both sides of each fish.
3 Mix together the lemon rind and juice, melted butter, parsley, and seasoning. Pour the mixture over the fish. Scatter the almonds over the top.
4 Cover the fish with foil and bake for 20–25 minutes, until the fish is cooked and the flesh flakes when tested with a fork.
5 Serve hot with sautéed potatoes and cooked fresh vegetables, such as peas and shredded green cabbage.

variations

- *Use mackerel or any other fish instead of trout.*
- *Use 2 limes or 1 orange instead of lemons.*
- *Use fresh chives or cilantro instead of parsley.*

fish *dishes*

braised chicken livers *with* apples

Tender oven-braised chicken livers are hard to beat when topped with apples and served with a tasty sauce. Liver is a good natural source of vitamin A, folic acid, and iron, all essential nutrients for healthy hair.

ingredients

- 1 tbsp olive oil
- 1 pound (450g) chicken livers, sliced
- 1 leek, washed and sliced
- 2 eating apples, peeled, cored, and thinly sliced
- 1 tbsp cornstarch
- ⅔ cup unsweetened apple juice
- ⅔ cup/¼ pint (150ml) vegetable stock (see recipe on page 20)
- 1 tbsp whole-grain mustard
- 1 tsp dried *herbes de provence*
- sea salt
- freshly ground black pepper
- fresh herb sprigs, to garnish

serves *four to six*
preparation time *20 minutes*
cooking time *20–30 minutes*

method

1 Preheat the oven to 375°F.
2 Heat the oil in a large nonstick skillet. Add the chicken livers and cook for 1–2 minutes, until sealed all over, turning once or twice. Using a spatula, remove the chicken livers from the skillet and place in an ovenproof dish. Cover and keep warm.
3 Add the leeks to the skillet and cook gently for 5 minutes, stirring occasionally. Spoon the leeks over the chicken livers and place the apple slices on top.
4 Blend the cornstarch with the apple juice and pour into the pan with the stock. Bring to a boil, stirring continuously, until the sauce thickens slightly. Simmer for 1 minute, stirring.

6 Stir in the mustard, dried herbs, and seasoning; then pour the sauce over the chicken liver mixture. Cover and bake for 20--25 minutes, until the chicken livers are cooked and tender.
7 Garnish with fresh herb sprigs and serve with cooked fresh vegetables such as new potatoes, sugar-snap peas, and baby zucchini.

variations

- *Use pears instead of apples.*
- *Use unsweetened grape juice instead of apple juice.*
- *Leave the apples unpeeled, if preferred.*

chicken *and* wild mushroom risotto

 Chicken and wild mushrooms add flavor to this appetizing risotto. Brown rice, in addition to containing dietary fiber, is an excellent source of magnesium, potassium, B vitamins and selenium.

ingredients

- 1 tbsp olive oil
- 8 ounces (225g) skinless, boneless chicken breast, cut into 1-inch (2.5cm) cubes
- 1 onion, chopped
- 1 large clove garlic, crushed
- 3 celery stalks, chopped
- 8 ounces (225g) mixed fresh wild mushrooms, such as shiitake and oyster mushrooms, sliced
- 1 cup/6 ounces (175g) frozen petit pois (baby peas)
- 1 7-ounce (200g) can corn kernels, drained
- 1¼ cups/8 ounces (225g) brown rice
- 1¾ cups/¾ pint (425ml) chicken stock (see recipe on page 20)
- 1¾ cups/¾ pint (425ml) dry white wine
- sea salt and ground black pepper
- 2–3 tbsp chopped fresh mixed herbs
- ¼ cup/1 ounce (25g) fresh, finely grated Parmesan cheese

serves *four to six*
preparation time *15 minutes*
cooking time *40 minutes*

method

1 Heat the oil in a large pan. Add the chicken and cook gently for about 5 minutes, until sealed all over, stirring frequently.

2 Stir in all the remaining ingredients, except the herbs and Parmesan cheese.

3 Bring to a boil; then reduce the heat and cook gently, uncovered, for about 35 minutes, until the rice and chicken are cooked and tender and almost all the liquid has been absorbed, stirring occasionally.

4 Stir in the mixed herbs and serve hot, sprinkled with the Parmesan cheese.

5 Serve with a tomato, bell pepper, and onion salad.

variations

- *Use turkey or lean lamb instead of chicken.*
- *Use cremini mushrooms instead of wild mushrooms.*
- *Use fresh tarragon or cilantro instead of mixed herbs.*

freezing instructions

Let cool completely, then transfer to a rigid, freezeproof container. Cover, seal, and label. Freeze for up to 3 months. Defrost completely, and reheat gently in a pan, adding a little extra stock, if necessary.

spiced tofu *and* carrot burgers

A tasty vegetarian alternative to meat, these spicy tofu burgers make a great snack or light meal. Tofu is an excellent source of protein and is rich in calcium, magnesium, folic acid, and iron—all of which are good hair nutrients.

ingredients

- 2tbsp olive oil
- 6 shallots, finely chopped
- 1½ cups/6 ounces (175g) coarsely grated carrots
- 1 clove garlic, crushed
- 1½tsp ground coriander
- 1½tsp ground cumin
- 1½tsp hot chili powder
- 12 ounces (350g) tofu, mashed
- ½ cup/2 ounces (55g) ground almonds
- ½ cup/2 ounces (55g) finely grated Cheddar cheese
- 1tbsp sun-dried tomato paste
- 1tbsp chopped fresh cilantro
- sea salt
- freshly ground black pepper

serves *four (two burgers each)*
preparation time *20 minutes*
cooking time *8 minutes*

method

1 Heat 1tbsp oil in a pan. Add the shallots, carrots, and garlic and cook over a medium heat for 4 minutes, stirring occasionally. Add the ground spices and cook for 1 minute, stirring.
2 Spoon the mixture into a bowl. Add the tofu, almonds, cheese, tomato paste, coriander, and seasoning and mix thoroughly. Cool slightly; then divide the mixture into eight portions and form each portion into a burger.
3 Preheat the broiler to high. Brush each burger all over with the remaining oil and place the burgers on a broiler rack in a broiler pan.
4 Broil for about 4 minutes on each side, until the burgers are cooked and lightly browned.
5 Serve hot with whole-wheat rolls, homemade relish or chutney, and a mixed leaf salad.

variations

- Use *finely chopped zucchini instead of carrots.*
- Use *hazelnuts instead of almonds.*

vegetable *dishes*

fruit *and* nut chewy bars

These chewy bars are ideal for a packed lunch. Dried fruits and oats provide dietary fiber and some essential hair nutrients.

ingredients

- ¾ cup/6 ounces (175g) butter
- ¾ cup/6 ounces (175g) light brown sugar
- 3tbsp maple syrup
- 3 cups/9 ounces (250g) rolled oats
- 2tsp ground cinnamon
- 1 cup/5 ounces (140g) mixed dried fruit such as golden raisins, raisins, and chopped dried apricots, and peaches
- ¾ cup/3 ounces (85g) chopped mixed almonds and hazelnuts

makes *16 bars*
preparation time *20 minutes*
cooking time *20–25 minutes*

method

1 Preheat the oven to 350°F.
2 Lightly grease a 7- x 11-inch cake pan.
3 Put the butter, sugar, and syrup in a pan and heat gently until melted, stirring occasionally. Remove from the heat.
4 Stir in the oats, cinnamon, dried fruit, and nuts.
5 Turn the mixture into the pan and press down to level the surface. Bake in the preheated oven for 20–25 minutes, or until golden brown.
6 Cut into bars while still warm and leave to cool completely in the pan.

variations

- *Use honey instead of maple syrup.*
- *Use ginger instead of cinnamon.*
- *Use cashews and Brazil nuts instead of almonds and hazelnuts.*

freezing instructions

Let cool completely, then wrap in foil or seal in a freezer bag and label. Freeze for up to 3 months. Defrost thoroughly for several hours at room temperature before serving.

desserts *and* bakes

banana *and* apricot compote

This simple compote of apricots and bananas is delicious served with low-fat yogurt. Bananas are easy to digest and are a good source of potassium and magnesium.

■ ingredients

- ¾ cup/7 fluid ounces (200ml) unsweetened apple juice
- ¾ cup/7 fluid ounces (200ml) unsweetened orange juice
- 4tbsp brandy
- 2tbsp honey
- 8 ounces (225g) dried apricots
- 2 cinnamon sticks, broken in half
- 6 whole cloves
- 4 firm, ripe bananas

serves *four*
preparation time *10 minutes*
cooking time *25 minutes*

■ method

1 Put the fruit juices, brandy, and honey in a pan and stir. Add the apricots, cinnamon sticks, and cloves and bring to a boil. Reduce the heat, cover, and simmer for 20 minutes, stirring occasionally. Remove the pan from the heat and discard the spices.

2 Peel and slice the bananas diagonally. Add to the pan and stir.

3 Serve the compote immediately, or set aside to cool and refrigerate before serving.

4 Serve with yogurt, crème fraîche, light sour cream, or frozen yogurt.

variations

• *Use unsweetened pineapple or grape juice instead of apple juice.*

• *Use chopped dried peaches, pears, or pineapple instead of apricots.*

• *Use sherry or rum instead of brandy.*

great *hair* day

INE YOUR WAY *to a healthier head of hair with delicious menu suggestions from the hair foods section—all include essential hair* nutrients. *Stress and pollution take their toll on our hair, so we need to ensure that we eat a well-balanced diet to help maintain shiny, luscious locks.*

spicy carrot *and* barley soup

Carrots provide carotenoids, which the body converts to vitamin A, an important nutrient for healthy hair.

ingredients

- 1 tbsp olive oil
- 1 onion, finely chopped
- 3 cups/1 pound (450g) finely chopped carrots
- 2 celery stalks, finely chopped
- ¼ cup/2 ounces (55g) pearl barley
- 2tsp ground cumin
- 2tsp ground coriander
- 1tsp hot chili powder (optional)
- 3½ cups/1½ pints (850ml) vegetable stock (see recipe on page 20)
- sea salt
- freshly ground black pepper
- fresh flat-leaf parsley, to garnish

serves *four*
preparation time *10 minutes*
cooking time *1¼ hours*

method

1 Heat the oil in a large pan. Add the onion and cook for 5 minutes, stirring occasionally.
2 Add the carrots, celery, pearl barley, and ground spices. Cook for 1 minute, stirring continuously. Stir in the stock.
3 Cover and bring to a boil; then reduce the heat and simmer for about 1¼ hours, stirring occasionally, until the barley is cooked and tender. Season to taste with salt and pepper.
4 Ladle into warmed soup bowls and garnish with chopped fresh flatleaf parsley.
5 Serve with whole-wheat bread.

chicken *and* wild mushroom risotto

Brown rice is an excellent source of magnesium, potassium, vitamins B$_3$ and E, folic acid, and selenium—will encourage a shining head of hair and healthy scalp.

ingredients

- 1 tbsp olive oil
- 8 ounces (225g) skinless, boneless chicken breast, cut into 1-inch (2.5cm) cubes
- 1 onion, chopped
- 1 large clove garlic, crushed
- 3 celery stalks, chopped
- 8 ounces (225g) mixed fresh wild mushrooms, such as shiitake and oyster mushrooms, sliced
- 1 cup/6 ounces (175g) frozen petit pois (baby peas)
- 1 7-ounce (200g) can corn kernels, drained
- 1¼ cups/8 ounces (225g) brown rice
- 1¾ cups/¾ pint (425ml) chicken stock (see recipe on page 20)
- 1¾ cups/¾ pint (425ml) dry white wine
- sea salt and ground black pepper
- 2–3tbsp chopped fresh mixed herbs
- ¼ cup/1 ounce (25g) fresh, finely grated, Parmesan cheese

serves *four to six*
preparation time *15 minutes*
cooking time *40 minutes*

method

1 Heat the oil in a large pan. Add the chicken and cook gently for about 5 minutes, until sealed all over, stirring frequently.
2 Stir in all the remaining ingredients, except the herbs and Parmesan cheese.
3 Bring to a boil; then reduce the heat and cook gently, uncovered, for about 35 minutes, until the rice and chicken are cooked and tender and almost all the liquid has been absorbed, stirring occasionally.
4 Stir in the mixed herbs and serve hot, sprinkled with the Parmesan cheese.
5 Serve with a tomato, bell pepper, and onion salad.

banana *and* apricot compote

Bananas are a good source of potassium, magnesium, and iron.

ingredients

- ¾ cup/7 fluid ounces (200ml) unsweetened apple juice
- ¾ cup/7 fluid ounces (200ml) unsweetened orange juice
- 4tbsp brandy
- 2tbsp honey
- 8 ounces (225g) dried apricots
- 2 cinnamon sticks, broken in half
- 6 whole cloves
- 4 firm, ripe bananas

serves *four*
preparation time *10 minutes*
cooking time *25 minutes*

method

1 Put the fruit juices, brandy, and honey in a pan and stir. Add the apricots, cinnamon sticks, and cloves and bring to a boil. Reduce the heat, cover, and simmer for 20 minutes, stirring occasionally. Remove the pan from the heat and discard the spices.
2 Peel and slice the bananas diagonally. Add to the pan and stir.
3 Serve the compote immediately, or set aside to cool and refrigerate before serving.
4 Serve with yogurt, crème fraîche, light sour cream, or frozen yogurt.

vision *foods*

FOODS THAT ARE *rich in vitamin A and beta carotene (the plant form of vitamin A), such as chicken liver, oily fish, carrots, spinach, and apricots, are essential for the eyes. A deficiency of vitamin A results in night blindness and dry eyes Insufficient* vitamin B_2 *can lead to inflamed eyelids and sensitivity to light. Vitamin B_2 is found in foods such as milk, yogurt, leafy green vegetables, eggs, meat, poultry, and fish. The omega-3 group of essential fatty acids, found in oily fish and walnuts, are also important for healthy eyes.*

mixed leaf *and* herb salad *with* grilled feta cheese

 This simple salad of mixed dark-green leaves and fresh herbs, topped with grilled feta cheese, makes a tasty appetizer. Spinach is rich in beta carotene, which is important for vision.

■ ingredients
- 4 ounces (115g) dark salad leaves such as baby spinach, watercress, and lollo rosso (coral lettuce)
- ¹⁄₂ cup/2 ounces (55g) watercress
- ¼ cup/¹⁄₂ ounce (15g) roughly torn or chopped fresh herbs such as parsley, basil, tarragon, mint, and chives
- 8 ounces (225g) cherry tomatoes, halved
- 1 tbsp olive oil
- 1 tbsp lemon juice
- 9 ounces (250g) feta or haloumi cheese, thinly sliced

for the dressing
- 3 tbsp walnut oil
- 2 tsp white wine vinegar
- 1 tsp honey
- 1 tsp Dijon mustard
- sea salt
- freshly ground black pepper

serves *four*
preparation time *15 minutes*
cooking time *6–8 minutes*

■ method
1 Put the salad leaves, watercress, herbs, and tomatoes in a bowl and toss together.
2 To make the dressing, put the walnut oil, vinegar, honey, mustard, and seasoning in a bowl and whisk together. Drizzle over the salad and toss. Divide the salad between four serving plates.
3 Preheat the broiler to high. Cover a broiler rack with foil. Mix together the olive oil and lemon juice and brush the feta or haloumi cheese with this mixture.
4 Place the cheese on the broiler rack and broil for 3–4 minutes each side, until lightly browned.
5 Top each salad with some cheese slices and serve immediately with thick slices of whole-wheat bread.

variations
- *Use arugula instead of watercress.*
- *Use olive oil or hazelnut oil instead of walnut oil.*
- *Use button mushrooms, halved, instead of tomatoes.*

soups *and* appetizers

mushroom *and* asparagus frittata

 This appetizing frittata makes a substantial first course or snack. Asparagus contains carotenoids, which are important for vision.

ingredients

- 4 ounces (115g) asparagus tips
- 1 tbsp/¹⁄₂ ounce (15g) butter
- 1 leek, washed and sliced
- 4 ounces (115g) cremini mushrooms, sliced
- 4 medium-sized eggs, beaten
- ¹⁄₂ cup/2 ounces (55g) grated Cheddar cheese
- sea salt
- freshly ground black pepper
- 2 tomatoes, peeled, seeded, and chopped
- fresh herb sprigs, to garnish

serves *two*
preparation time *10 minutes*
cooking time *15 minutes*

method

1 Cook the asparagus in a pan of boiling water for about 2 minutes, until cooked and tender. Drain well and keep warm.

2 Melt the butter in a medium-sized nonstick skillet. Add the leeks and mushrooms and cook gently for 8–10 minutes, until softened, stirring occasionally.

3 Preheat the broiler to high. Pour the eggs over the vegetables in the skillet, sprinkle over the cheese and seasoning, and stir briefly.

4 Cook over medium heat for a few minutes, until cooked and golden brown underneath.

5 Put under the broiler for a few minutes to brown the top.

6 Scatter the asparagus and tomatoes over the top and serve—on its own or with slices of whole-wheat bread or toast. Garnish with herb sprigs.

variations

- Add 1 tbsp chopped fresh or 1 tsp dried mixed herbs with the eggs.
- Use sliced zucchini instead of asparagus.
- Use 1 onion instead of the leek.
- Use ¹⁄₄–¹⁄₂ cup/1–2 ounces (25–55g) fresh Parmesan cheese instead of Cheddar cheese.

barbecued mackerel *with* mustard sauce

This barbecued fish with a tasty mustard sauce is good for eating alfresco. Oily fish such as mackerel contain omega-3 fatty acids and vitamin A, which help to protect cell membranes.

■ ingredients

- 2 eating apples, peeled, cored, and thinly sliced
- 3tbsp chopped fresh parsley
- sea salt
- freshly ground black pepper
- 4 mackerel, each weighing 10–12 ounces (280–350g), gutted and cleaned
- juice of 2 lemons

for the sauce

- 2tbsp cornstarch
- 1¼ cups/½ pint (300ml) milk
- 1tbsp whole-grain mustard
- 1tbsp/½ ounce (15g) butter
- fresh parsley sprigs, to garnish

serves *four*
preparation time *15 minutes*
cooking time *20–30 minutes*

■ method

1 Light the barbecue and leave until the coals are hot enough to cook over.

2 Lightly grease four sheets of foil, each large enough to hold a fish in a package.

3 Mix the apples, 2tbsp chopped parsley, and seasoning. Spoon the mixture into the fish cavities.

4 Place one fish on each piece of foil and sprinkle with a little lemon juice; then fold the foil over the fish and twist the edges to secure, making four packages.

5 Put the packages over the coals and cook for 20–30 minutes, until the fish is cooked and the flesh flakes when tested with a fork.

6 Meanwhile, make the sauce. In a pan, blend the cornstarch with a little milk. Stir in the remaining milk; then heat, stirring continuously, until the sauce comes to a boil and thickens slightly.

7 Stir in the mustard, butter, seasoning, and remaining chopped parsley. Heat gently until piping hot, stirring continuously.

8 Unwrap the foil packages, place the cooked fish on warmed serving plates, and garnish with fresh parsley sprigs. Pour some mustard sauce over each fish.

9 Serve hot with baked potatoes, and broiled bell peppers and eggplants.

variations

- *Add an extra 1tbsp whole-grain mustard to the sauce if you prefer a slightly stronger mustard flavor.*
- *Use trout instead of mackerel.*
- *Use pears instead of apples.*
- *Use 1–2tbsp finely chopped capers instead of mustard.*

fish

pan-fried squid *with* chili sauce

Fresh squid, pan-fried and tossed in a hot chili sauce, makes a tasty lunch dish. Squid is a low-fat source of protein that contains many important nutrients. Chilies are an excellent source of vitamin C.

■ ingredients

- 1 14-ounce (400g) can chopped tomatoes
- 2 shallots, finely chopped
- 2 celery stalks, finely chopped
- 1 fresh red chili, seeded and finely chopped
- 1 clove garlic, crushed
- ²/₃ cup/¹/₄ pint (150ml) dry white wine
- 1 tbsp tomato paste
- sea salt
- freshly ground black pepper
- 2 tbsp (30ml) olive oil
- 2 pounds (900g) prepared squid, cut into rings

serves *four to six*
Preparation time *10 minutes*
Cooking time *3–5 minutes*

■ method

1 Put the tomatoes, shallots, celery, chili, garlic, wine, tomato purée, and seasoning in a small pan and stir.

2 Bring the mixture to a boil; then reduce the heat to medium and cook, uncovered, for 15–20 minutes, until the sauce is cooked and thickened, stirring occasionally.

3 Meanwhile, heat the olive oil in a nonstick wok or large skillet. Add the squid and stir-fry over a high heat for about 5 minutes, until tender.

4 Toss the cooked squid and chili sauce together and serve hot with lightly buttered whole-wheat bread and a mixed bell pepper and onion salad.

variations

• *Use red wine or unsweetened apple juice instead of white wine.*
• *Use 1–2 tsp hot chili powder instead of the fresh chili.*
• *Use 1 pound (450g) fresh tomatoes, peeled and chopped, instead of canned tomatoes.*

chicken livers *with* Madeira sauce

Chicken liver is an excellent natural source of vitamins A and B$_{12}$, folate, and iron, but since it's also high in fat and cholesterol, we save it for special occasions.

ingredients

- 1 tbsp olive oil
- 6 shallots, sliced
- 1 pound (450g) chicken livers, cut into thin strips
- 4 tbsp vegetable stock (see recipe on page 20)
- 4 tbsp Madeira
- 1 tsp dried *herbes de provence*
- 2 tbsp crème fraîche or light sour cream
- sea salt
- freshly ground black pepper
- fresh herb sprigs, to garnish

serves *four to six*
preparation time *10 minutes*
cooking time *12 minutes*

method

1 Heat the oil in a large nonstick skillet. Add the shallots and cook for 5 minutes, stirring.

2 Add the chicken livers and cook over a medium to high heat for 5 minutes, stirring frequently.

3 Add the stock, Madeira, and dried herbs. Bring the mixture to a boil and cook for 2 minutes, until the chicken livers are cooked and tender, stirring frequently.

4 Stir in the crème fraîche or light sour cream and seasoning. Reheat gently until piping hot, stirring.

5 Garnish with fresh herb sprigs. Serve hot with boiled mixed brown and wild rice and cooked fresh vegetables such as broccoli florets and green beans.

variations

• *Use 1 onion instead of the shallots.*

• *Use red wine instead of Madeira.*

meat *and* poultry *dishes*

chicken *and* broccoli pasta bake

This tasty pasta bake makes an appetizing meal for the whole family to enjoy. Broccoli is rich in beta carotene (the plant form of vitamin A), making it excellent for healthy eyes. Chicken is a good source of vitamin B_2.

ingredients

- 8 ounces (225g) pasta shapes
- 8 ounces (225g) small broccoli florets
- 2 zucchini, sliced
- 1 leek, washed and sliced
- 1/4 cup/2 ounces (55g) butter
- 1/2 cup/2 ounces (55g) plain whole-wheat flour
- 2 1/2 cups/1 pint (600ml) chicken stock (see recipe on page 20), cooled
- 1 1/4 cups/1/2 pint (300ml) milk
- 1 cup/4 ounces (115g) grated Cheddar cheese
- 1 3/4 cups/8 ounces (225g) diced, cooked, skinless, boneless chicken
- 2tbsp chopped fresh chives
- 1tbsp chopped fresh parsley
- sea salt
- freshly ground black pepper
- 2tbsp finely grated fresh Parmesan cheese
- fresh parsley sprigs, to garnish

serves *four to six*
preparation time *20 minutes*
cooking time *25–30 minutes*

method

1 Preheat the oven to 400°F.
2 Cook the pasta in a large pan of lightly salted, boiling water for about 8 minutes, until just tender. Rinse, drain well, and keep warm.
3 Meanwhile, steam the broccoli, zucchini, and leeks over a pan of boiling water for about 10 minutes, until just cooked and tender. Drain well and keep warm.
4 Put the butter, flour, stock, and milk in a pan and heat gently, whisking continuously, until the sauce comes to a boil and thickens. Simmer gently for 2 minutes, stirring.
5 Remove the pan from the heat and stir in the Cheddar cheese, chicken, chopped herbs, and seasoning. Add the pasta and vegetables and mix well.

6 Spoon the mixture into an ovenproof dish and sprinkle the Parmesan cheese over the top. Bake, uncovered, for 25–30 minutes, until golden brown.
7 Garnish with the parsley sprigs and serve with broiled tomatoes and bell peppers.

variations
• *Use cooked turkey or cooked, flaked salmon or tuna instead of chicken.*
• *Use cauliflower florets or sliced mushrooms instead of broccoli.*
• *Use 1 onion instead of the leek.*

freezing instructions
Let cool completely, then transfer to a rigid, freezeproof container. Cover, seal, and label. Freeze for up to 3 months. Defrost for several hours, or overnight in the refrigerator. Reheat in the oven.

meat *and* poultry *dishes*

frizzling sweet potato wedges *with* sesame seeds

These frizzling sweet potato wedges sprinkled with sesame seeds are a tasty accompaniment to many dishes. Sesame seeds are rich in essential fatty acids, and add a little zinc, potassium, magnesium, and iron to the diet.

ingredients

- 1 1/2 pounds (700g) red-fleshed sweet potatoes
- 1 tbsp olive oil
- 1 tbsp/1/2 ounce (15g) butter
- 2 tbsp toasted sesame seeds
- 2 tbsp chopped fresh chives
- sea salt
- freshly ground black pepper

serves *four*
preparation time *10 minutes*
cooking time *11–16 minutes*

method

1 Peel the potatoes and cut them into wedges. Parboil in a pan of boiling water for 5 minutes. Drain thoroughly.

2 Heat the oil and butter in a nonstick skillet until the butter has melted. Add the potatoes and cook over a medium heat for about 10–15 minutes, turning occasionally, until the potatoes are cooked, lightly browned, and crisp all over.

3 Add the sesame seeds and cook gently for 1–2 minutes; then stir in the chives and seasoning.

4 Serve hot with broiled lean meat or fish and cooked vegetables, such as spinach and leeks.

variations

- *Use potatoes, parsnips, or rutabaga instead of sweet potatoes.*
- *Use sesame oil instead of olive oil.*
- *Use sunflower or pumpkin seeds instead of sesame seeds.*
- *Use chopped fresh mixed herbs instead of chives.*

vegetable *dishes*

country bean goulash

This hearty goulash is full of nutrients and makes a warming meal. Beans and legumes are rich in vitamin B₂, a nutrient that may help prevent cataracts. The vitamin C in tomatoes and bell peppers may also have cataract-preventing properties.

ingredients

- 3 cups/1½ pounds (700g) peeled, seeded, and chopped tomatoes
- 1 onion, chopped
- 1 large clove garlic, finely chopped
- 1 red bell pepper, seeded and diced
- 3 carrots, sliced
- 3 celery stalks, chopped
- 6 ounces (175g) button mushrooms
- 1 cup/6 ounces (175g) frozen peas
- 1 14-ounce (400g) can red kidney beans, rinsed and drained
- 1 14-ounce (400g) can black-eyed peas, rinsed and drained
- 1¼ cups/½ pint (300ml) medium sweet cider
- 2tbsp paprika
- 2tsp dried *herbes de provence*
- sea salt
- freshly ground black pepper
- 1tbsp cornstarch
- fresh herb sprigs, to garnish

serves *four to six*
preparation time *15 minutes*
cooking time *1½ hours*

method

1 Preheat the oven to 350°F.
2 Put all the ingredients, except the cornstarch and herb garnish, in a large flameproof, ovenproof casserole and stir.
3 Bake in the preheated oven for about 1½ hours, until the vegetables are cooked and tender, stirring occasionally. Remove from the oven.
4 Blend the cornstarch with 4tbsp water. Stir into the vegetable mixture, then heat gently on the stove top, stirring continuously, until the mixture comes to a boil and thickens slightly. Simmer gently for 2 minutes, stirring.
5 Serve the bean and vegetable goulash hot with brown rice, noodles, or couscous. Garnish with fresh herb sprigs.

variations
· Use unsweetened apple juice instead of cider.
· Use peas instead of broad beans.
· Use a 14-ounce (400g) can chopped tomatoes instead of fresh tomatoes.

freezing instructions
Let cool completely, then transfer to a rigid, freezeproof container. Cover, seal, and label. Freeze for up to 3 months. Defrost and reheat gently in a pan or moderate oven.

vegetable *dishes*

apricot yogurt crush

This yogurt crush, with its delicate fruity flavor, makes a delicious light dessert. Yogurt is rich in vitamins B$_1$ and B$_2$ and provides easily digestible protein as well as magnesium, potassium, zinc, and vitamin A—vital nutrients for healthy eyes.

ingredients

- 1 14-ounce (400g) can apricots in fruit juice
- 1 7-ounce (200g) can apricots in fruit juice
- 1¼ cups/11 ounces (300g) plain yogurt
- ⅔ cup/¼ pint (150ml) light cream
- 2tbsp honey
- fresh mint sprigs, to decorate

serves *six*
preparation time *10 minutes, plus freezing time*

method

1 Blend the apricots and juice in a food processor until smooth.
2 Add the yogurt, cream, and honey, and blend until well mixed. Pour into a chilled, shallow, plastic container. Cover and freeze for 1½–2 hours or until the mixture is mushy in consistency.
3 Spoon into a bowl and mash with a fork until smooth. Return to the container, cover, and freeze until firm.
4 Transfer to the refrigerator 30 minutes before serving to let the yogurt ice soften a little. Serve in scoops and decorate with fresh mint sprigs.
5 Serve with mixed fresh berries such as strawberries, raspberries, blueberries, and blackberries.

variations
• *Use canned peaches or pineapple instead of apricots.*
• *Use crème fraîche instead of light cream.*
• *Use maple syrup instead of honey.*

blueberry *and* apple crunch

The tasty combination of blueberries and apples makes this crunchy nut crumble hard to resist. Blueberries are a great eye food because they provide vitamin C and other antioxidants, which are essential to eye health.

ingredients

- 1 cup/4 ounces (115g) whole-wheat flour
- 1 cup/3 ounces (85g) medium oatmeal
- ⅓ cup/3 ounces (85g) butter
- ⅓ cup/3 ounces (85g) light brown sugar
- 2 ounces (55g) chopped mixed almonds and Brazil nuts
- 1tsp ground cinnamon
- 12 ounces (350g) blueberries
- 5 eating apples, peeled, cored, and thinly sliced
- 3tbsp unsweetened apple juice
- 3tbsp honey

serves *four to six*
preparation time *20 minutes*
cooking time *45 minutes*

method

1 Preheat the oven to 350°F.
2 Mix the flour and oatmeal in a bowl, then lightly rub in the butter until the mixture resembles coarse bread crumbs. Stir in the sugar, nuts, and cinnamon.
3 Put the blueberries and apples in an ovenproof dish. Mix together the apple juice and honey and pour over the fruit. Stir.
4 Spoon the crumble mixture evenly over the fruit.
5 Bake in the preheated oven for about 45 minutes, or until the fruit is cooked and the topping is golden brown and crunchy.
6 Serve hot or cold with homemade custard sauce or yogurt.

variations
• *Use fresh mixed berries such as raspberries and blackberries, instead of blueberries.*
• *Use rolled oats instead of oatmeal.*
• *Use brandy or sherry instead of apple juice.*

desserts *and* bakes

a *feast* for the *eye*

SEEING IS BELIEVING—*you can have your Blueberry and Apple Crunch and eat it too! Just feast your eyes on this nutritious selection of* recipes from the vision foods section. These recipes provide vitamins A (via beta carotene) and B_2, so dig in for healthier eyesight!

mixed leaf *and* herb salad *with* grilled feta cheese

Spinach is a good source of vitamin B_2 and beta carotene—important for vision.

ingredients

- 4 ounces (115g) dark salad leaves such as baby spinach, watercress, and lollo rosso (coral lettuce)
- ½ cup/2 ounces (55g) watercress
- ¼ cup/½ ounce (15g) roughly torn or chopped fresh herbs such as parsley, basil, tarragon, mint, and chives
- 8 ounces (225g) cherry tomatoes, halved
- 1 tbsp olive oil
- 1 tbsp lemon juice
- 9 ounces (250g) feta or haloumi cheese, thinly sliced

for the dressing

- 3 tbsp walnut oil
- 2 tsp white wine vinegar
- 1 tsp honey
- 1 tsp Dijon mustard
- sea salt
- freshly ground black pepper

serves *four*
preparation time *15 minutes*
cooking time *6–8 minutes*

method

1 Put the salad leaves, watercress, herbs, and tomatoes in a bowl and toss together.

2 To make the dressing, put the walnut oil, vinegar, honey, mustard, and seasoning in a bowl and whisk together. Drizzle over the salad and toss. Divide the salad between four serving plates.

3 Preheat the broiler to high. Cover a broiler rack with foil. Mix together the olive oil and lemon juice and brush the feta or haloumi cheese with this mixture.

4 Place the cheese on the broiler rack and broil for 3–4 minutes each side, until lightly browned.

5 Top each salad with some cheese slices and serve immediately with thick slices of whole-wheat bread.

country bean goulash

Beans and legumes are rich in vitamin B_2—a nutrient that may help prevent cataracts.

ingredients

- 3 cups/1½ pounds (700g) peeled, seeded, and chopped tomatoes
- 1 onion, chopped
- 1 large clove garlic, finely chopped
- 1 red bell pepper, seeded and diced
- 3 carrots, sliced
- 3 celery stalks, chopped
- 6 ounces (175g) button mushrooms
- 1 cup/6 ounces (175g) frozen peas
- 1 14-ounce (400g) can red kidney beans, rinsed and drained

- 1 14-ounce (400g) can black-eyed peas, rinsed and drained
- 1¼ cups/½ pint (300ml) medium sweet cider
- 2tbsp paprika
- 2tsp dried *herbes de provence*
- sea salt
- freshly ground black pepper
- 1tbsp cornstarch
- fresh herb sprigs, to garnish

serves *four to six*
preparation time *15 minutes*
cooking time *1½ hours*

▌ method

1 Preheat the oven to 350°F.

2 Put all the ingredients, except the cornstarch and herb garnish, in a large flameproof, ovenproof casserole and stir.

3 Bake in the preheated oven for about 1½ hours, until the vegetables are cooked and tender, stirring occasionally. Remove from the oven.

4 Blend the cornstarch with 4tbsp water. Stir into the vegetable mixture, then heat gently on the stove top, stirring continuously, until the mixture comes to a boil and thickens slightly. Simmer gently for 2 minutes, stirring.

5 Serve the bean and vegetable goulash hot with brown rice, noodles, or couscous. Garnish with the herb sprigs.

blueberry *and* apple crunch

Blueberries provide vitamin C and other antioxidants, which are essential to eye health.

▌ ingredients

- 1 cup/4 ounces (115g) whole-wheat flour
- 1 cup/3 ounces (85g) medium oatmeal
- ⅓ cup/3 ounces (85g) butter
- ⅓ cup/3 ounces (85g) light brown sugar
- 2 ounces (55g) chopped mixed almonds and Brazil nuts
- 1tsp ground cinnamon
- 12 ounces (350g) blueberries
- 5 eating apples, peeled, cored, and thinly sliced
- 3tbsp unsweetened apple juice
- 3tbsp honey

serves *four to six*
preparation time *20 minutes*
cooking time *45 minutes*

▌ method

1 Preheat the oven to 350°F.

2 Mix the flour and oatmeal in a bowl, then lightly rub in the butter until the mixture resembles coarse bread crumbs. Stir in the sugar, nuts, and cinnamon.

3 Put the blueberries and apples in an ovenproof dish. Mix together the apple juice and honey and pour over the fruit. Stir.

4 Spoon the crumble mixture evenly over the fruit.

5 Bake in the preheated oven for about 45 minutes, or until the fruit is cooked and the topping is golden brown and crunchy.

6 Serve hot or cold with homemade custard sauce or yogurt.

which body problem *needs which* food?

immune system problems

• Foods high in vitamin E, such as vegetable oils, leafy green vegetables, whole grains, nuts, and seeds help protect the immune system.

• When you feel a cold coming on, make a hot drink with lemon juice, a small piece of fresh root ginger and a teaspoon of honey. The lemon juice is rich in vitamin C, the ginger is warming and the honey soothes the throat.

• Garlic and onions may be helpful in alleviating nasal congestion.

teeth and bone problems

• Help to prevent tooth decay by finishing a meal with foods that do not harm your teeth. Cheese is thought to protect dental enamel by reducing mouth acidity.

• Bleeding gums can be a sign of vitamin C deficiency. Include plenty of fresh fruit and vegetables in your diet.

• Eating plenty of calcium- and magnesium-rich foods, plus doing weight-bearing exercise, is the best way of preventing or minimising osteoporosis.

joint problems

• People who suffer from osteoarthritis should improve their diet by eating more whole-grain cereals, fresh fruit and vegetables, to increase their intake of antioxidants.

• Fish oils may prove helpful to people who suffer from rheumatoid arthritis. Salmon, trout, mackerel, and tuna all contain omega-3 fatty acids, which may have an anti-inflammatory effect on the joints of some arthritis sufferers.

• Painful joints can sometimes be caused by an intolerance to certain foods.

heart and circulation problems

• A diet high in whole grains, fruit, and vegetables helps to lower cholesterol.

• Fats from oily fish such as salmon, trout, mackerel, and tuna can help to prevent blood clots forming in the arteries.

• Garlic and onions may help to lower blood pressure and cholesterol levels.

• If you suffer from high blood pressure, limit the amount of salt you have in your diet.

problem *solving*

which beauty problem
needs which food?

skin problems

- If you have a skin rash or hives, or suffer from eczema, it may signal an allergy to particular foods. Common allergens are milk products, nuts, citrus fruits, tomatoes, fish and shellfish, eggs, and wheat The only way that such an allergy can be confirmed is by means of an elimination diet.
- For flaking skin, include plenty of essential fatty acids in your diet.
- If you have sensitive skin, or cracks and sores around your mouth, eat plenty of foods rich in B vitamins.
- Dabbing fresh lemon juice onto the skin and massaging it in with a little extra virgin olive oil is good for improving skin condition and reducing wrinkles.
- Psoriasis sufferers may benefit from including intake oily fish in their diet, for more omega-3 fatty acids.

nail problems

- If you have brittle, flaking nails, include plenty of essential fatty acids in your diet.
- Pale, brittle nails and itchy skin may indicate iron deficiency. Good sources of iron include meat, dark-meat poultry, enriched breads and cereals, and green leafy vegetables.
- Brittle nails, infections of the surrounding skin, or white marks on the fingernails may indicate zinc deficiency. Zinc-rich foods include seafood, eggs, liver, nuts, lentils, and garbanzo beans.

hair problems

- Dry scalp and dandruff may indicate a deficiency of zinc, so eat plenty of seafood, eggs, liver, nuts, lentils, and garbanzo beans. Essential fatty acids, found in oily fish and nuts, also help a dry scalp and dry hair.
- Dull hair may indicate a lack of vitamin A. For beta carotene (the plant form of vitamin A), ensure your diet includes plenty of carrots, dark-green leafy vegetables, and dried apricots.

eye problems

- The risk of cataracts and an age-related eye condition known an macular degeneration may be reduced by eating plenty of green leafy vegetables.
- If you suffer from conjunctivitis or bloodshot eyes, make sure you are getting enough Vitamin B_2—found in meat, eggs, milk, cheese, yogurt, legumes, and green leafy vegetables.
- Poor vision in the dark may be a sign of a deficiency of vitamin A. Ensure your diet includes plenty of carrots, dark-green leafy vegetables, and dried apricots.

problem *solving*

vitamins *and* minerals

FOODS CONTAIN DIFFERENT *levels of nutrients, and no single food can provide all the nutrients needed for good health. Vitamins and minerals found in foods work synergistically with proteins, carbohydrates, fats, and each other. To make sure you ingest sufficient nutrients, vary your diet as much as possible. The following lists are a guide to recommended daily nutrition requirements.*

Fat-soluble vitamins

vitamin A
from retinol in animal products and beta carotene in plant foods
Essential for growth and cell development, vision, immune function. Maintains healthy skin, hair, nails, bones, and teeth.

vitamin D
calciferols
Needed for calcium absorption; helps build and maintain strong bones and teeth.

vitamin E
tocopherols
Protects fatty acids; maintains muscles and red blood cells; a major antioxidant.

vitamin K
phylloquinone, menaquinone
Essential for proper blood clotting.

Water-soluble vitamins

biotin
Needed to release energy from food and for the synthesis of fat and cholesterol.

folic acid
folate, folacin
Needed for cell division and formation of DNA, RNA, and proteins. Extra needed before conception and in pregnancy to guard against neural tube defects.

vitamin B$_1$
thiamin
Needed to obtain energy from carbohydrates, fats, and alcohol; supports nerve function.

vitamin B$_2$
riboflavin
Needed to release energy from food and to assist the functioning of vitamin B$_6$ and niacin.

vitamin B$_3$
niacin, nicotine acid, nicotinamide
Needed to produce energy in cells. Helps to maintain healthy skin and an efficient digestive system.

vitamin B$_5$
pantothenic acid
Helps to release energy from food. Essential to the synthesis of cholesterol, fat and red blood cells.

vitamin B$_6$
pyridoxine, pyridoxamine, pyridoxal
Help to release energy from proteins; important for immune function, the nervous system, and the formation of red blood cells.

vitamin B$_{12}$
cyanocobalamin
Needed to make red blood cells, DNA, RNA, and myelin (for nerve fibers).

vitamin C
ascorbic acid
Vitamin C is a major antioxidant, vital for healthy immune function, and for the production of collagen (a protein essential for healthy gums, teeth, bones, cartilage, and skin. It also aids the absorption of plant food.

Minerals

calcium
Builds strong bones and teeth; vital to muscle and nerve function, and blood clotting.

chloride
Maintains proper body chemistry. Used to make digestive juices.

chromium
Helps to regulate blood sugar levels and blood cholesterol levels and reduces cravings for junk foods.

copper
Needed for bone growth and connective tissue formation. It helps the body to absorb iron from food and is present in many enzymes that protect against free radicals.

iodine
Necessary for the manufacture of thyroid hormones.

iron
Needed for the manufacture of red blood cells and for energy production within cells.

magnesium
Stimulates bone growth, assists in nerve impulses, and is important for muscle contraction.

manganese
Vital component of various enzymes involved in energy production; helps to form bone and connective tissue.

molybdenum
Essential component of enzymes involved in the production of DNA and RNA; may fight tooth decay.

potassium
Helps to regulate the body's fluid balance and distribution to keep the heartbeat regular and maintain normal blood pressure. It is important for muscle and nerve function.

phosphorus
Helps maintain strong bones and teeth. However, in excess (such as results from excessive consumption of fizzy drinks) it affects the body's ability to use calcium and magnesium.

selenium
A major antioxidant that works with vitamin E to protect cell membranes from damage due to oxidation.

sodium
Works with potassium to regulate the body's fluid balance; essential for proper nerve and muscle function.

sulfur
Component of two essential amino acids that help to form many proteins in the body.

zinc
Essential for normal growth, reproduction, and immune function.

vitamins

US/CANADA

Recommended Dietary Allowances/Recommended Nutrient Intakes

(for adults over 24)

	MALES	FEMALES
Vitamin A	1000mcgR.E./1000mcgR.E.	800mcgR.E./800mcgR.E.
Vitamin D	5mcg/2.5mcg	5mcg/2.5mcg
Vitamin E	10mg/9mg	8mg/6mg
Vitamin K	80mcg/80mcg	65mcg/65mcg
Biotin	30–100mcg*/30–100mcg†	30–100mcg*/30–100mcg†
Folic acid	200mcg/230mcg	180mcg/185mcg
Vitamin B3	19mg/19mg	15mg/14mg
Vitamin B5	4–7mg*/4–7mg†	4–7mg*/4–7mg†
Vitamin B2	1.7mg/1.4mg	1.3mg/1mg
Vitamin B1	1.5mg/1.1mg	1.1mg/0.8mg
Vitamin B6	2mg/2mg†	1.6mg/1.6mg†
Vitamin B12	2mcg/1mcg	2mcg/1mcg
Vitamin C	60mg/40mg	60mg/40mg

* RDAs have not been established: values for these minerals are based on current expert opinion.
† RNIs have not been established: values for these minerals are based on current expert opinion.

minerals

US/CANADA

Recommended Dietary Allowances/Recommended Nutrient Intakes

(for adults over 24)

	MALES	FEMALES
Calcium	800mg/800mg	800mg/800mcg (1000–1500mg after menopause)
Magnesium	350mg/250mg	280mg/200mg
Phosphorus	800mg/1000mg	800mg/850mg
Chromium	0.05–0.2mg*/0.05–0.2mg†	0.05–0.2mg*/0.05–0.2mg†
Copper	1.5–3mg*/2–3mg†	1.5–3mg*/2–3mg†
Iodine	150mcg/160mcg	150mcg/160mcg
Iron	10mg/9mg	15mg/9–13mg
Manganese	2.5–5mg*/2.5–5mg†	2.5–5mg*/2.5–5mg†
Selenium	70mcg/70mcg	55mcg/55mcg
Zinc	15mg/12mg	12mg/9mg
Potassium	1875–5625mg*/2–6g†	1875–5625mg*/2–6g†
Sodium	1100–3300mg*/1–3g†	1100–3300mg*/1–3g†

* RDAs have not been established: values for these minerals are based on current expert opinion.
† RNIs have not been established: values for these minerals are based on current expert opinion.

index

acknowledgments

Grateful thanks to Dr. Udo Erasmus from Canada for his facts on essential fats, and in the UK, the Institute of Optimum Nutrition and Patrick Holford, and nutritionist Gareth Zeal for their support.

Hazel Courteney

Many people have worked very hard to prepare this book. My respect and admiration must go, in particular, to Hazel Courteney, and to Anne Sheasby who created the sumptuous store of recipes. It has been a pleasure to work with such conscientious and caring professionals.

Kathryn Marsden

I would like to thank Robert for his on-going support and encouragement with this book and for his tireless tasting of all the recipes; Kathryn Marsden for all her help and advice; Anne Townley and Viv Croot for asking me to create all the recipes for this book; and Molly Perham and Caroline Earle for all their hard editing work.

Anne Sheasby